R59787

745.44959
GAN

BASIC IBAN DESIGN

KV-382-891

WITHDRAWN FROM STOCK

BASIC IBAN DESIGN

AN INTRODUCTION

By
Augustine Anggat Ganjing

Translation
By
Gana Ngadi

This book is a translation of an Iban manuscript entitled
Batang Jalai Ngukir written by Mr. Augustine Anggat Ganjing

Dewan Bahasa dan Pustaka
Ministry of Education
Kuala Lumpur
2001

This book is published by Dewan Bahasa dan Pustaka, Sarawak Branch, with the cooperation of the General Publication Division, Dewan Bahasa dan Pustaka, Kuala Lumpur.

First Printing 1988
Second Printing 2001
© Augustine Anggat Ganjing 1988

All Rights Reserved. No part of this book may be reproduced or transmitted in any form or by any means, electronic or mechanical, including photocopying, recording, or any information storage and retrieval system, without permission in writing form the Director-General, Dewan Bahasa dan Pustaka, P.O. Box 10803, 50926 Kuala Lumpur, Malaysia. Negotiation is subjected to the calculation of royalty or honorarium.

Perpustakaan Negara Malaysia   Cataloguing-in-Publication Data

Augustine Anggat Ganjing, 1947-
    Basic Iban design : an introduction / Augustine Anggat Ganjing ;
    translation by Gana Ngadi.
    ISBN 983-62-0272-2
    1.   Carving (Decorative arts)--Sarawak. 2. Design--Sarawak.
    2.   Decoration and ornament--Sarawak. I. Gana Ngadi.
    II. Title.
    747.44959522

Printed by
Percetakan Dewan Bahasa dan Pustaka
Lot 1037, Mukim Perindustrian PKNS
Ampang/Hulu Kelang
Selangor Darul Ehsan

Dedicated to my wife
Marilyn Mandah Seli
and
to the peoples of Sarawak.

CONTENTS

ACKNOWLEDGEMENT

FIRST of all I must acknowledge the help given to me by the former Curator of the Sarawak Museum, the late Mr. Benedict Sandin, K.M.N., P.B.S., who kindly permitted me to make observations and take photographs of the various designs found in his residence, and also for the various advice and encouragement given to me. Encouragement was also given by the present Director of the Sarawak Museum Mr. Lucas Chin, P.B.S., P.P.B., who permitted me to utilise the services of the then Museum photographer, Encik Ahmad Junaidi bin Latif, to photograph relevant designs or objects found in the Museum for this book.

I am also grateful to Mr. John S. Daley, a former member of the Voluntary Service Abroad from New Zealand, and Mr. Anthony Ahim, a photographer of the Department of Agriculture, who took photographs of some valuable designs for me during the course of their extensive travelling throughout Sarawak. Special thanks also go to Mr. Yee, an Assistant Artist, and Encik Ewandi Jong, both from the Department of Agriculture, who spent much of their time in assisting me to take some photographs for the purpose of compiling this book.

Finally, my most heartful thanks and appreciation to the late Lemambang (the bard) Ganjing anak Ayu, for contributing various legends and making authoritative comments on designs. Without the assistance and advice of those mentioned above, I would not have been able to produce this work.

AUGUSTINE ANGGAT GANJING

INTRODUCTION

How was design first discovered among the Dayaks, especially the Ibans, Kayans and Kenyahs? Was it derived from the dreams of their ancestors? Was it formed from their forefathers' thoughts? Was it formed from the yearning for beautiful ornaments? Was it derived from their gods who looked after them? Was it because they wanted to follow the hobbies of the dwellers of the world of *Panggau Libau,* the home of war gods namely Keling, Laja, Sempurai and others, which was believed to be beautifully decorated with unique designs. Was it copied from foreign lands by our ancestors?

What were the actual uses of the designs? Were they used to frighten off the enemies, especially the designs made on shields? Were the shield designs meant to attract the attention of an adversary during combat, thus catching him off-guard? Were they meant to show the ingenuity of the designers concerned thereby receiving appreciation and praises from the people? Were they aimed at protecting families from diseases and illnesses? Were they meant to be used as a form of writing to help remember the many chants and invocations? Were they meant to bring luck in farming and trading or for obtaining better offsprings, preferably males? Were they meant as symbols for the rich and the glorious? Were they meant to advance the Iban culture in the field of designing, including that of body tattooing; or increase the knowledge acquired from the Kelabits and the Kenyahs who are also skilful designers?

Some legends say that the Ibans are able designers because their gods wished them to be so. Some say that their designs originated from gods such as *Keling Gerasi Nading Bujang Berani Kempang, Laja Mirah Moa Nekang*

Jerenang, Simpurai Muntigerai, Sepatu Manok Antu, Sepungga Lumpong Nangga, Pandak Segatak and others. These are the gods of war who live in the Kingdom of Panggau Libau, which is believed to be a beautiful and unique place. Other than the Ibans, Kayans and Kenyahs, the Melanaus are also expert designers. Their skill and perseverance in the art of designing can be seen on the posts of their houses. Melanau designs are not very much different from that of the Ibans.

According to Iban belief, those who do not belong to the upper class or those who are in poverty, are not allowed to decorate their rooms with designs of dragon, human being, tiger or giant forms. Any violation of this prohibition can bring ruin to the offenders.

It is also considered harmful to have dragon designs facing the onlooker. Thus such designs are often found applied sideways, with symbolic designs of the creature's food made right in front of it. Dragon designs are normally made in a pair, one facing the other. This is to enable each dragon to have a meal-time companion as well as having a friend to 'converse' with, thereby causing no 'disturbance'.

If those who do not belong to the upper class, or are not well off make designs of human beings on the walls of their houses, it is believed that their houses will be burnt down. The tiger designs must also be applied sideways, together with the designs of its food. The design of the figure of a giant must not be made in the room of person belonging to the lower class otherwise misfortunes will befall him. Such designs are preferably done on shields, for it is believed that they will make the Ibans more courageous and render the enemies frightened of helpless. It is also suitable to design it on the girth of a notched tree trunk ladder, to 'protect' the occupants of the longhouse from evil spirits.

Dayak designs always originate from the forms of such animals as deer, barking deer, wild boar, dog, monkey and bear. Significant birds such as the rhinoceros hornbill and pheasants are also featured.

In making a hornbill carving, it is generally considered taboo for the caver to carry out the entire work by himself, from the start to the finish. However, if the carver is a prominent authority such an undertaking will not bring forth any ill-effect.

It is my opinion that the art of designing reflects Dayak appreciation of the beautiful things surrounding them. The designs also symbolise a sense of close rapport and mutual help amongst the Dayaks themselves, be it in times of joy or distress. The Dayaks do not possess their own writing. As a result, the designs represent one of the ways by which their identity can be portrayed. There are certain differences between designs done by Dayaks and non-Dayaks. For example, the Dayaks make unique designs on knife handles and scabbards, shields, paddles and boats' bows. Peculiar designs are also found in their weaving, basketwork and many others. Special designs are made, too, on the ritual houses for the dead at their graveyards, as a mark of great respect to their ancestors who guided and protected them from their enemies, and had provided them with land and dwelling places.

Designs reflect Dayak skill and ingenuity to the world, as is the case with the Maoris of New Zealand. The Maoris are carvers of very high standing. Their sophisticated designs can be seen on the walls, posts and doors of their houses.

This is an example of a Maori face tattoo.

In the middle of the Celebes Island in Indonesia, there is a group of people called the *Torajas*. They are fond of making designs of the walls, posts, ladders and other parts of their houses. The *Torajas* are also fond of carving human and animal figures from wood.

Not far from Jerantut, in Peninsular Malaysia, there is a community called the *Jah Hut*. The *Jah Huts* are also fond of carving human, animal and other figures. Sometimes these figures are planted in the forests to ward off evil spirits. Other than carving human figures they also make designs of their musical instruments, kitchen utensils and other tools. Here is an example of a carved figure made by the *Jah Huts*.

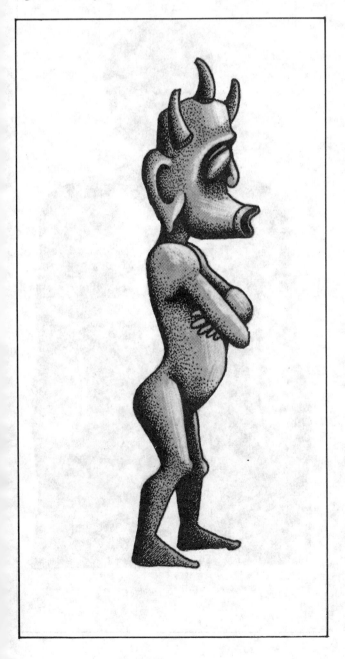

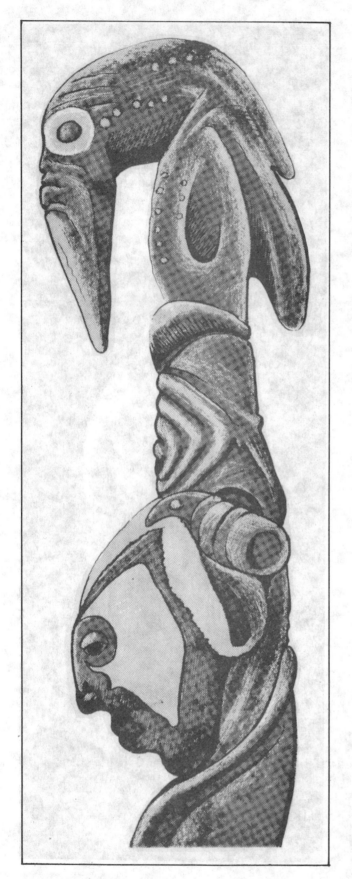

The photograph on the left shows the figure of a type of hornbill placed on top of a human head. It was made by a group of natives of Papua, New Guinea. It symbolises that god created both man and bird and they are to live in co-existence.

The picture below shows the Iban 'Kelingai' tattoo. The 'Kelingai' seen on the back of this old man is known as 'Bunga Terung', which means 'Brinjal Flower'. Immediately below the nape of his neck is found the 'Ketam Ngerayap' (Crawling Crab) designs.

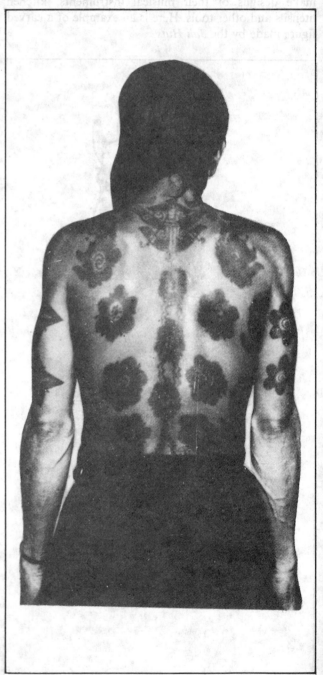

We should appreciate this unique skill which we have inherited from our ancestors. This uniqueness portrays part of our social foundation, and should be studied seriously by the younger generation. Such designs are not only meant for decorating scabbards, for example, but also for beautifying the walls and posts of our houses.

I am contributing my part in helping to develop and further the growth of this aspect of our cultural heritage. In this book I attempt to explain my knowledge of the art of designing through illustrations and elucidations. There are many experts in this field and the methods of designing may vary. The methods so described in this book are based on my own research, approach and techniques.

My aim in writing this book is to provide some guidelines for the younger generation, many of whom have never seen an expert carver or designer at work, and on how to begin and finish a piece of carving or design. In conclusion, it is my hope that the future generations will value and perpetuate this knowledge.

RITUAL CHANT-BOARD (PAPAN TURAI)

The ritual chant patterns are designed according to the sequence of the ritual chant (*Pengap*) in order that the ritual chant expert (*Lemambang*) will not miss the steps of the chant. The designs in the chant-board represent various places and names of certain gods mentioned in the chant. One should not omit or allow the proper sequence of the chants, to be mixed up otherwise the spirits of the invited gods will not come to the festival. The place of 'Aki Ungkok' (Grandfather Ungkok who is believed to inhabit the moon) looks like this.

The types of pattern used in the chant-board may vary from division to division, or perhaps from district to district. The chant board shown here belongs to Lemambang Ayu and his followers, namely Lemambang Ganjing, Lemambang Mulok, Lemambang Bundan and Lemambang Juing, all from Simunjan District, First Division, Sarawak.

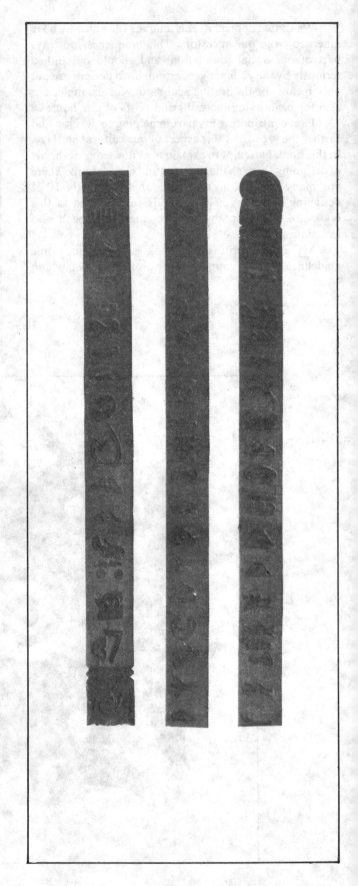

Design: *'Lua Genali Bekaul Kaki'*

CHAPTER I

THE ORIGIN OF DESIGNS

RAWING AND RAJA MEROM

ONCE upon a time, when Raja Merom heard about the strength and courage of a man named Rawing he commanded his warriors to capture Rawing, for fear that the latter's power would surpass his own. Through guiles and trickery, Rawing was captured while still sleeping, and brought over to Raja Merom's palace. When he woke up he noticed that he was in a strange place. He then realised that he had been captured but he did not know who his captors were.

Rawing went outside the palace where he encountered Raja Merom, who then laughed uproariously upon seeing him. Before Rawing could say anything, Raja Merom exclaimed: "Rawing, you are now my prisoner, but do not be sad because I shall make you the head of all the other prisoners. You shall be more powerful than them, and your food shall be as good as mine. You shall lead and direct the prisoners at their work, but you shall not be paid. What do you have to say, do you agree?"

Rawing took a long time to consider Raja Merom's suggestion. As he was given special food together with a fine place to sleep in, and as he was a good a kind-hearted person, he finally agreed to Raja Merom's command. In the meantime, he would think of a plan to overcome his plight.

As promised by Raja Merom, the food given to Rawing was always excellent, in fact many times better than that received at home. It was the same, too, with his bedroom. However, Rawing still felt miserable because he lived apart from his parents. Even though his room was excellent and clean, it was devoid of any form of decoration. "If I apply suitable designs to the walls of this room, I am sure it will become even more beautiful than it is now," Rawing thought.

Without further ado, Rawing immediately drew beautiful designs on the walls of the room. On the left wall he made designs of human figures. To the right were designs of dragons, while on the rear wall were drawn tigers. The front part of the wall was decorated with designs of hornbills. Rawing was an expert designer. The exquisite beauty of his designs was beyond description.

When Raja Merom entered the room he was mesmerized by the designs. Without saying a word, he retreated to his palace and immediately instructed his men to obtain paints of various colours. He then ordered Rawing to make designs on the walls of his room as well as within the entire palace. From that day onward, Rawing did not do any other work except designing.

When all the walls of every room in the palace were decorated with designs, Raja Merom was so pleased with the beauty and splendour of his palace that he asked

Raja Merom was mesmerized by Rawing's designs.

Rawing to name his fee. Rawing requested for his freedom as payment, as he missed his family very much. Raja Merom consented. He was convinced that Rawing did not have any feeling of vengeance against him. That night, Raja Merom held a grand ceremony to show his satisfaction with the designs, and also to bid Rawing farewell. Many of his subjects, including prisoners, were invited. The guests were also entertained to various performances during the ceremony.

Before Rawing's departure the next day, Raja Merom rewarded him with five gantangs of gold coins and a ship. With the gold Rawing bought gongs and various musical instruments made from brass and copper. Raja Merom and Rawing promised to help each other in times of trouble, especially if attacked by their enemies.

When Rawing's ship arrived at his village port the people were both greatly surprised and afraid. They thought that an enemy ship was coming to attack them, but when the ship berthed at the wharf they realised that it was none other than Rawing. Rawing's parents were very happy to see him again. They were also extremely overjoyed to notice that he had brought back a lot of valuables with him.

This is a story of how the skill in designing was used to free oneself from captivity.

Kuda Taṣik (Sea-horse)

LANG NGINDANG AND LANG KACHANG

Long ago, when the country was in turmoil, designs helped to scare as well as weaken one's enemy during combat.

There was once a war leader by the name of Lang Ngindang who was engaged in mortal combat with another war leader called Lang Kachang. Both of them were equally strong and brave. Each held a very well-designed war shield. They had fought for a long time but neither could manage to cut down the other as both were exceptionally skilful, as quick as lightning and as agile as a butterfly.

After some time both warriors felt very tired. They rested behind the protection of their own war shields. Their sweat poured out in rivulets to wet the earth. Their warcoats were wet and their sword handles felt slippery. The bushes growing around them were flattened. Leaves and roots were scattered here and there as if they had been plucked or uprooted.

While resting on the battle ground to overcome their fatigue, the visions of both the war leaders became brighter again. Lang Ngindang was quick to observe the designs done on the war shield of his opponent, Lang Kachang. He was awestruck by the exquisite beauty of the designs made on the shield that he forgot they were foes. He felt as if he was in a dream. The longer he looked at the designs on Lang Kachang's war shield, the lesser were his feelings of animosity for Lang Kachang. If Lang Kachang had risen up there and then to attack him, he was certain that he would not be nimble enough to pick up his parang which had slipped through his fingers a short while ago.

Strangely, at that same moment Lang Kachang was also observing the designs done on Lang Ngindang's war shield. While doing so, Lang Kachang became so frightened that his hair stood on ends. The longer he rested his eyes on Lang Ngindang's war shield, the more frightened he became. He felt as if his head was swelling to the size of a large *takin* (a small type of basket). As he was extremely frightened, Lang Kachang retreated and fled. He was followed by his men.

Lang Ngindang was perplexed by his opponent's behaviour. He commanded his followers to cease fighting. From that day onwards, both war leaders did not fight each other any more.

Lang Ngindang and Lang Kachang looking at each other's
shield.

Pasun Nyalak (i)
(A giant's barking dog)

GEMONG'S DREAM

THE Ibans do not possess a writing of their own. The bards (ritual chants experts) make use of various carved designs on pieces of chanting boards to help them remember the sequences of the chants while chanting. These chanting boards are called *papan pengap* or *papan turai.*

Some people are of the opinion that certain Iban designs had their origin in a dream as told in the following story:

A long time ago, there lived an old man by the name of Gemong. One day, while on his way home from the padi-field, Gemong was caught in a heavy rain. Drenched, Gemong shivered with cold. At home he warmed himself in front of the fireplace. After a while Gemong yawned several times and soon fell asleep. He then had a dream; feeling as if he was walking on the verandah of a longhouse. There he saw that the walls, posts, pestles and mortars, rice-grinders, knife scabbards and handles, mats, large baskets *(lanji)* and many other objects all bore beautiful designs. Even the sticks used for chasing away the chickens had designs on them. All the males in the longhouse had their bodies tattooed, too.

The intricate and beautiful designs amazed Gemong. Then an old man appeared beside him and told him of the various names of the designs. The old man also elaborated on the methods of executing the designs. Then he brought Gemong into each room in the longhouse. Each room had a different style of design done to its walls. Upon entering the chief's room, Gemong observed that the walls were filled with various designs which were grander and more exquisite than those found in other rooms. The left wall was filled with dragon designs, while the right wall displayed the hornbill designs. The back wall bore tiger designs, contrasting with that of the front which had designs or human forms. Gemong was so enthralled that he could not leave the chief's room. Such was his feeling that he broke into a dance. While dancing thus in his dream his foot accidentally kicked against the burning firewood on the hearth nearby. It woke him up.

Gemong then started designing on the walls of his house, memorising the designs as seen by him in his dream. It is believed that a good number of the Iban designs available today originated from those done by Gemong.

Gemong in a dream.

Pasun Nyalak (ii)
(A giant's barking dog)

BUBUT (CONTROCOCCYX) AND RUAI
(ARGUS PHEASANT) SPIRITS

SOME people are of the opinion that Iban ability for the art of designing stemmed from the designs found on the Bubut bird.

One day, two men by the names of Nyanggau and Jantau went into the jungle to tap *jelutong* trees for latex. At that time, *jelutong* rubber fetched a high price. After spending some time in the jungle they decided to hunt, as they had not taken meat for a long time.

Shortly after they had started hunting, their dog started to bark at a very big wild boar. The wild boar halted in its tracks, poised to fight against the dogs. Being the most agile of the two, Nyanggau dashed forward first and managed to stab the wild boar with his spear. Somehow his spear became stuck in the wild boar, which carried it off. Nyanggau and Jantau then started tracking the animal. They tracked downriver, criss-crossing hills and valleys. They only managed to find the dead wild boar towards late evening. It fell between two buttresses of a large tree. Realising that they had strayed too far from their camp, Nyanggau and Jantau decided to spend the night in that place.

While Nyanggau and Jantau were about to roast the wild boar, two strangers passed by. The two men invited them to their house, which was not too far away. Nyanggau and Jantau accepted as they had not brought any food along with them.

Unknown to them the two strangers were actually the Spirits of the *Bubut* (Controcaccyx) and the *Ruai* (Argus Pheasant) birds in human forms.

Upon reaching the house, Nyanggau and Jantau stood transfixed when they noticed that it was beautifully decorated with various designs. These appeared everywhere, both outside and inside the house. Not an inch was spared. They were an industrious pair, and their love for designing grew to such an extent that all the posts and ladders of their house, including their pots and various water containers, were covered with beautiful designs. Nyanggau, Jantau and their hosts stayed up late that night, conversing on a wide variety of subjects.

Early next morning Nyanggau and Jantau decided to leave but the Bubut and Ruai spirits pressed them to stay longer, as there was still so much for them to discuss. Realising that their hosts were really sincere, Nyanggau and Jantau agreed to stay on. Throughout their sojourn there, Nyanggau and Jantau assisted in padi farming and hunting. In the evenings they learned craftsmanship like carving and binding. Both the Bubut and Ruai spirits were skilful in craftsmanship. They lived together like brothers, and never once did they quarrel. They were also extremely kind to Nyanggau and Jantau.

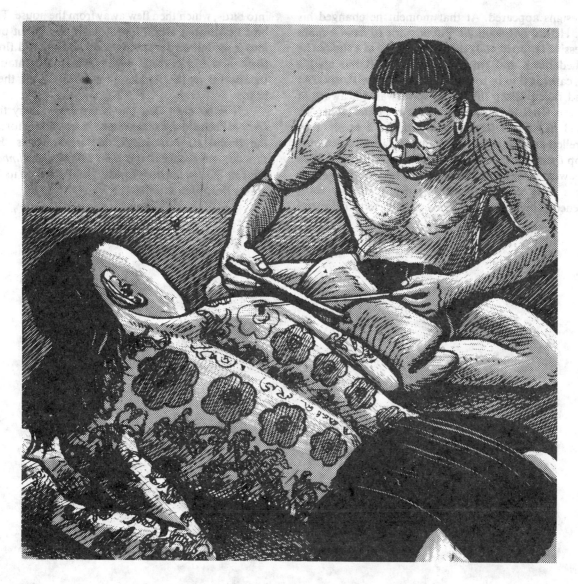

The Bubut spirit tattooing the Ruai spirit.

After a time, the Bubut and Ruai spirits decided to tattoo each other's body. They went into the jungle to look for the correct herbs, for brewing the colours needed for tattooing. After getting everything ready, they discussed as to who would be tattooed first.

"I do not mind who is first," said the Bubut spirit, "after all, we are all expert designers."

"Very well. Let me be the first one to be tattooed. I am anxious to see how smart I would appear with a tattooed body," replied the Ruai spirit.

"Jantau and I will follow whatever has been suggested. Even if you do not wish to tattoo us we will not be disappointed," stressed Nyanggau.

Without further ado the Ruai spirit stretched out his body for the Bubut spirit to tattoo him. The Bubut spirit

began his work in the morning and did not finish until noon time. As soon as he finished, the Ruai spirit rushed eagerly to the river to see his reflection in the water. Realising how very smart he looked, he felt extremely happy, and uttered *"Umbau Wai!"* meaning, "It is enough, my friend!" He uttered this repeatedly. The designs suited his face and body and were very well done. Both Jantau and Nyanggau were equally happy to see how beautiful the Ruai spirit looked.

It was already approaching noon and all of them were hungry. While taking his food, the Ruai spirit kept on admiring his tattooed body, for he was extremely proud of it.

After lunch it was the Ruai spirit's turn to tattoo the Bubut spirit. Half way through he noticed how beautiful

13

the designs appeared. At that moment he changed his mind. He did not want the Bubut spirit to have a more impressive tattooed body than himself. All of a sudden he splashed black and red paints over the Bubut spirit's body, causing it to be coloured black with red streaks. As he had fallen asleep the Bubut spirit was not aware of what the Ruai spirit had done to him. Later, when he realised it, he was terribly annoyed. As a result, they quarrelled and fought. Nyanggau and Jantau attempted to stop them but to no avail as both the Bubut and Ruai spirits were stronger than the two of them put together. After a long and pertinacious fight, a strange thing happened. The Bubut and Ruai spirits were transformed into birds, which then flew away from the house. The Ruai bird flew into a virgin forest, while the Bubut bird flew into a secondary forest. As soon as they had flown off, their house vanished. Nyanggau and Jantau found themselves in the middle of a forest. They then went home.

It is believed that this is the reason why the Ruai (Argus Pheasant) is seldom seen in secondary forests, and the Bubut (Contrococcyx) in virgin forests. Even to this day we can hear the *Ruai* calling out *Umbau Wai! Umbau Wai!* in the deep forest. The designs on its feathers are as beautiful as ever.

Bunga Terung Dua Betunga

BUNTAK ALOI AND BUNTAK RUSA

ACCORDING to Iban belief the godly world of Panggau Libau is a famous place where its inhabitants are always happy and contented. Among the others, Keling Gerasi Nading and Laja Tampak Mua, who were also held in high esteem, lived in Panggau Libau.

One day, while in the prime of their bachelorhood, Keling and Laja decided to visit a godly longhouse known as Gelong Batu Nakong, with the intention of meeting two beautiful maidens by the names of Kumang and Lulong. Both donned their finest warriors' outfits. They adorned head-dresses which were beautifully decorated with myriads of relief patterns. Their outfits also included the *subak* dress, whose patterns resembled the shell of the *kepayang* seed. They were armed with swords and shields.

After completing the necessary preparations, both Keling and Laja opened the doors of the rooms, made from the buttress roots of the *tapang* tree. Then they walked through the longhouse and down the staircase, simultaneously grasping the staircase railing, made from the *purang* wood. Keling and Laja crossed a bridge that seemed to have no ending, then walked through the *sabang seluang* grove (a type of plant which is normally used in Iban ceremonial rites). Whenever they felt themselves swaying to the right, because of exhaustion, they held onto their blowpipes, made from the *tapang* wood. When swaying to the left, they stopped themselves from falling by holding onto their knife handles which were made from deer horns. They walked swiftly, as swift as released darts and flew like butterflies until they reached a deserted wide path.

Upon reaching a place where water was available, Keling and Laja did not even stop to dive. They crossed turbid waterfalls whose cascading waters sounded like the throbs of small gongs. They walked so swiftly that roots were uprooted, dried leaves flew up and scattered here and there, and buttress roots broke. By leaps and bounds, the two young warriors strode over the *empili* tree, the place where wild boar meat was usually roasted.

Here they witnessed a wild boar, long dead, suddenly came back to life and root the soil again. Keling and Laja also passed through flatlands that were grown with *ijok* (a type of palm). This was the place where the deer meat was usually smoked. Although a mousedeer had been long killed, they saw it coming back to life to reach out for the fruits of the *buan* tree.

Later, Keling and Laja passed through a hill overgrown with the *salak* tree. It was the place where venison was usually preserved. Here a strange thing occurred. Although the deer had already been cut up into many pieces, it miraculously rose up and leapt away.

Towards late afternoon, Keling and Laja heard human voices and cock crows coming from the direction of Gelong Batu Nakong.

"Let us disguise ourselves as old men," suggested Keling.

"I will follow whatever you say, Buat," replied Laja.

They strode to the *jelutong* tree which stood alongside a *pelai* tree, made several cuts on both trees, then debbed themselves with the latex, thus making their faces appear wizened and ugly. The warts growing on their skin!" they commented. However, some invited ringworm scars resembled insect wings. Mucus trickled down from their noses. Their teeth were either broken or sharp-pointed and their perspiration stank.

When they reached the bathing place of the Gelong longhouse, the bathers were revolted at the sight of Keling and Laja.

"How ugly their features are, and look at the sores on their skins!" they commented. However, some invited Keling and Laja to join them in the river. Others kept quiet, for fear that they might just join them. However, Keling and Laja declined their invitation saying that they were not feeling well.

As soon as they reached the longhouse, Keling and Laja went straight to Ngelai's room. Ngelai was wellknown in Gelong Batu Nakong for his kind-heartedness towards people, regardless of their look or origin. Keling introduced himself as 'Buntak Aloi' and Laja as 'Buntak Rusa'.

One day, both Keling and Laja were told by Ngelai to keep watch over the padi being dried. However, the 'old' men only looked after the padi, and allowed the chickens to run freely and peck at the padi seeds.

When Ngelai came he saw the chickens pecking at the padi. "Oh dear! Why didn't you chase away the chicken?" exclaimed Ngelai. "They will certainly eat up all the padi if left unattended. You have to beat them to make them go away."

"Oh ... is it done that way?" Keling asked. Later, they started beating the chickens until many of them died. Those that survived suffered from broken legs and wings. The dead chickens were scattered here and there.

Feeling uneasy Ngelai went to the padi drying platform. "Oh dear! Now many of the chickens are killed by them. Those two old men are certainly weird."

Ngelai's wife commented, "You do not have to beat the chicken, you only need to drive them off, that's all."

"Oh! So that's the way, cousin Ngelai. But only a short while ago you instructed us to beat them," answered Laja.

During their stay in Gelong Batu Nakong, Keling and Laja went courting almost every night. 'Buntak Aloi' or Keling courted Kumang, while 'Buntak Rusa' or Laja courted Lulong. When they went to see the maidens, the

Buntak Aloi and Buntak Rusa keeping watch over the padi.

'masks' which caused them to look hideous were taken off and left with a female slave by the name of Indai Lipai. With their 'masks' discarded, Keling and Laja looked their normal selves; both were extremely handsome and dignified.

Before Keling and Laja arrived at Gelong Batu Nakong, Kumang was usually courted by Gelayan Ragak Riang. The youthful Gelayan was from Gelong Batu Nakong itself. Although he was a strong and handsome man, Gelayan could not be compared to Keling or Laja.

Keling and Laja thus regularly continued courting Kumang and Lulong. After one such visit Kumang presented Keling with a ring as a token of her affection. Indirectly she was also hoping to discover the true identity of her young suitor. When Keling returned to Ngelai's

longhouse, he mischievously slipped the ring into the sleeping Ngelai's finger. When Ngelai woke up, he was immensely astonished to discover a ring on his finger. He was more angry when the ring could not be slipped out of his finger. What was peculiar was that the ring appeared to be loose when he straightened his finger but became stuck when he attempted to take it off!

When Kumang observed the ring on Ngelai's finger, she immediately thought that Ngelai was the one who was courting her. However she could not believe that Ngelai would make fun of her thus. Every morning she checked all the junctions located near her longhouse to detect the route used by her suitor. She came across a certain path but the entrance of the path as covered by cobwebs. It was the same, too, with other paths. Kumang was truly perplexed as to the true identity of her dashing

17

Buntak Aloi and Buntak Rusa carving the hornbill images. Someone commented that the images looked like the carvers themselves.

suitor. On the other hand, Lulong, through her magical powers, knew who their secret admirers were. However, she did not wish to reveal the knowledge to Kumang at that time.

After Keling and Laja had stayed in Gelong Batu Nakong for quite some time, the elders decided to hold the *Gawai Kenyalang* ritual festival. A month before the festival, the people started to carve the ritual wooden hornbill images. Each family had to make one for the occasion. The wooden image of the hornbill had to be carved elaborately. Those who did not acquire the art of carving the hornbill wooden image had to seek assistance from the ones who could. So it came about that Kumang and Lulong requested Buntak Aloi (Keling) and Buntak Rusa (Laja) to carve the hornbill wooden images for their families.

About five days before the festival began, each carving of the wooden hornbill image was completed and placed on a tray. This was in turn placed on a special platform. All the carvings were absolutely exquisite, especially that carved by Gelayan Ragak Riang. Gelayan was appointed to carve the main wooden hornbill image which would later be mounted atop a tall festival pole during the *Gawai Kenyalang*. Gelayan boasted that he was a very skilful carver and could handle handicraft of various sorts. He sneered at the wooden hornbill images carved by Buntak Aloi and Buntak Rusa. Although theirs were allowed to be placed on the tray and covered with a woven blanket, he considered them incomplete. Someone commented that the images looked like the carvers themselves.

The big day eventually came. The carvers concerned were asked to exhibit their wooden hornbill images to the crowd. The last persons to reveal their exhibits before Gelayan were Buntak Aloi and Buntak Rusa. The crowd gathered closer as they were about to show their carvings. Their main purpose was not so much as to see the carvings but rather to make fun of the two 'old' men.

Strangely, as soon as Buntak Rusa uncovered his exhibit, out flew the wooden hornbill image. The same also happened to Buntak Aloi's wooden hornbill image. It flapped its wings and flew until it reached the door of Kumang's room. The wooden images were covered with designs never before seen by the people. In terms of intricacies and beauty, the carvings were beyond their imagination. Some of them tried to catch the wooden images because they thought that they were real hornbills. Kumang and Lulong were overjoyed. When Gelayan finally uncovered his hornbill image, it appeared ugly, not as it had looked before.

The Gelong Batu Nakong dwellers were taken aback. Some began to think that Buntak Aloi and Buntak Rusa were no ordinary mortals. Realising the situation, Buntak Aloi and Buntak Rusa then took off their 'masks', which had made them appear hideously old all that time. Instantly both of them appeared very handsome and dignified. It was only then that the crowd realised that the two 'old men' were really Keling and Laja, two famous youths of Panggau Libau. As soon as the festival was over, Keling married Kumang and Laja married Lulong.

From this legend, it is believed that some designs originated from the gods who reside in Panggau Libau and Gelong Batu Nakong.

Bunga Terung Empat Betentang

CHAPTER 2

LEAVES AND JORQUETTES OF DESIGN

TYPES OF DESIGN

THE designs here are classified into two main types: the Balanced Type and the Unbalanced Type. In the Balanced Type, the jorquette which includes the branches and the leaves on the right side are similar to those on the left. For example, if the jorquette on the right contains four leaves and two branches, the jorquette on the left will also contain four leaves and two branches. In short, the right portion is always similar to that on the left.

In the Unbalanced Type, the jorquette on the right side is different from that on the left. For example, if the jorquette on the right contains four leaves and two branches, the jorquette on the left may contain only three or five leaves and one branch, or probably may not contain any branch at all, or even may not contain any jorquette at all.

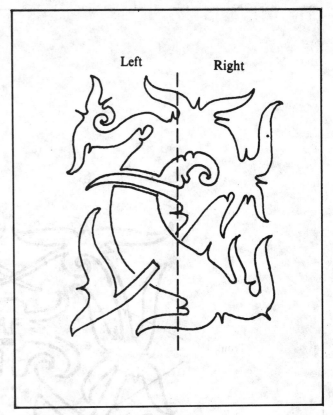

Unbalanced Type (Irregular)
Note that the right portion is entirely different from that of the left.

NAMES OF PARTS OF DESIGN

The Balanced and the Unbalanced Types of design can be subdivided into four parts, namely the base, the trunk, the jorquette and the leaves. When combined together, all these parts are known as the feature or body of the designs. The designs are said to be based on animal, bird, human, dragon and giant forms. The methods of beginning and elaborating the designs will be explained in Chapter Three.

The main body, be it of animal, bird or snake form, is called the base of the design from where the actual design evolves. The extra branches sprouting from the jorquette is called **chupon.** The creeper that branches out from the base of the design and connected to the jorquette is called the **trunk** of the design. The base where the trunks meet or branch out is known as the **jorquette.** The short branch or shoot issuing from the jorquette is called the **leaf** of the particular design.

'Chupons' are commonly found in irregular types of design and *Kelingai.* The 'chupon' serves as a substitute for the leaves and branches. In an area which is unsuitable for either a leaf or a branch to be drawn, a 'chupon' may become the best substitute.

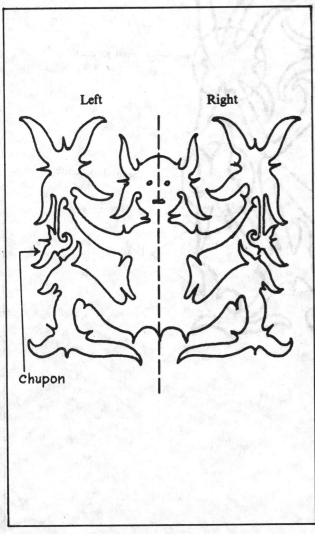

Balanced Type (Regular)
The jorquette on the top right has four leaves, the same as that found on the top left.

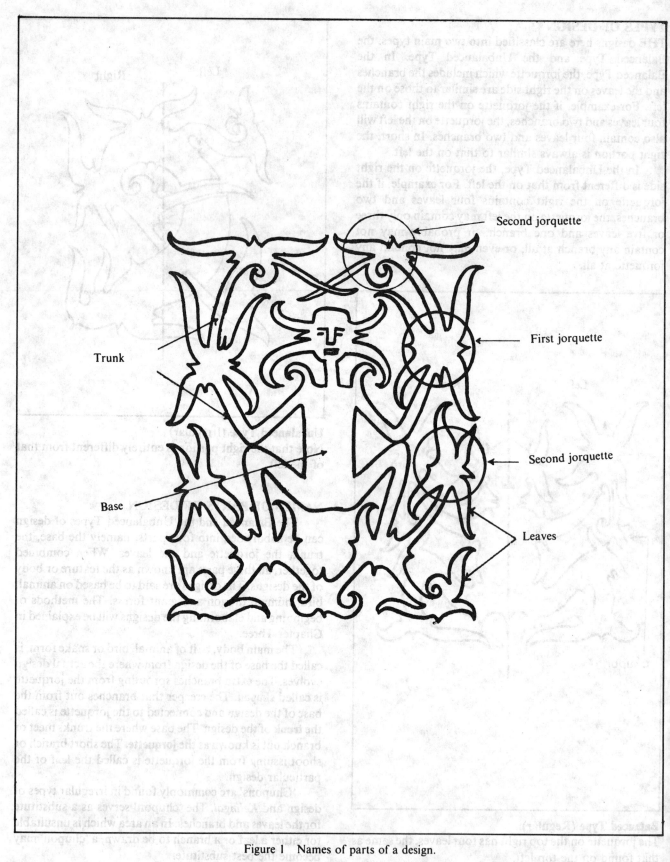

Second jorquette

First jorquette

Trunk

Second jorquette

Base

Leaves

Figure 1   Names of parts of a design.

The most important part from the four parts of designs as mentioned are the jorquette and the leaves of designs. Thus each designer must be adept at designing these. The jorquette patterns vary and all of them cannot be elaborated here. The choice is left to the individual designer.

The jorquette patterns to be applied also depend very much on the availability of space and the types of design intended. For instance, to execute designs on a knife handle as shown below, every space and corner must be utilised so that the patterns will appear regular and ornate. Therefore designers must know how to apply the proper jorquette patterns and the leaves of designs.

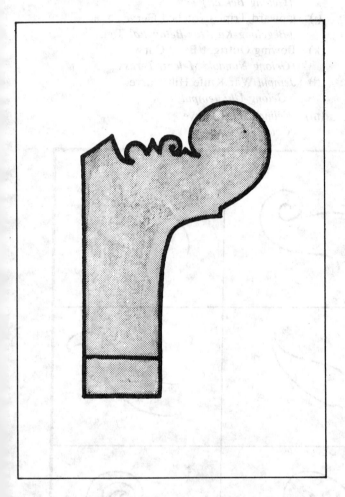

Figure 2   Knife handle before it is designed.

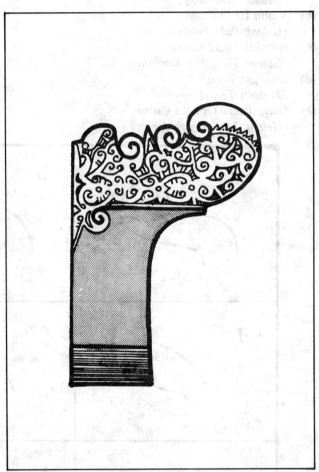

Figure 3   Knife handle after it has been designed.

LEAVES OF DESIGN

Below are show some patterns of the leaves of designs.
These serve as guidelines to beginners.

Leaves of Designs
(a) *Lemiding* Fern Curve
 (Gelong Lemiding)
(b) Violin Head Curve
 (Gelong Pala Belula)
(c) Hornbill Head Curve
 (Gelong Tangkong Kenyalang)
(d) Outright Bend
 (Melenti Terus)
(e) Sharp Point Upright Curve
 (Gelong Enchanggak Juring)

(f) Return Curve
 (Gelong Nikal)
(g) Bowing Curve
 (Gelong Nundok)
(h) Double-Notched Bowing Curve
 (Gelong Nundok Betangkal Dua)
(i) Interlocking Curve
 (Gelong Bekaul)
(j) Upward Triple-Notched Curve
 (Begelong Ka Atas Betangkal Tiga)
(k) Bowing Outright Bend Curve
 (Gelong Nundok Melenti Terus)
(l) *Jempul* War Knife Hilt Curve
 (Gelong Ulu Jempul)
(m) *Kelindu* Fern Curve
 (Gelong Kelindu)

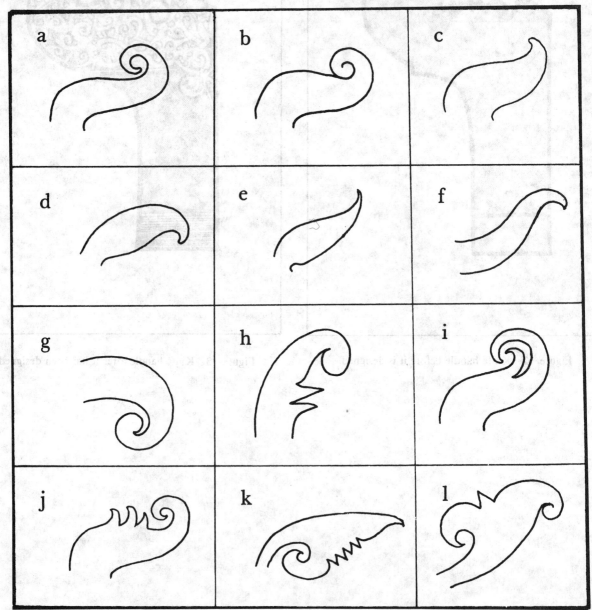

(n) *Kubok* Fern Curve
  (Gelong Kubok)

(o) *Demam* Fern Curve
  (Gelong Demam)

(p) Wild Betel Leaf Curve
  (Gelong Sirih Abap)

(q) Bear Claw Curve
  (Gelong Kukut Beruang)

(r) Beak Curve
  (Gelong Betangkong)

(s) Spur Curve
  (Gelong Tada)

(t) *Semunjing* Curve
  (Gelong Semunjing)

(u) Bowing and Upraised Curve
  (Gelong Nundok Ngelentik Ka Atas)

(v) Grasping Curve
  (Gelong Ngenggam)

(w) *Bunga Tapang Bubut* Curve
  (Gelong Bunga Tapang Bubut)

(x) *Kubok* Fern Outright Bend
  (Gelong Kubok Melenti Terus)

(y) *Sikat-ikat* Curve
  (Gelong Sikat-ikat)

(z) Prawn's Spear Curve
  (Gelong Undai)

(za) Upright Curve With Three Tips
  (Gelong Enchanggak Bechunggit Tiga)

m	n	o
p	q	r
s	t	u
v	w	x
y	z	za

After observing the patterns of the leaves of designs, we are then able to envisage the prime importance of each leaf design. It is necessary to know which leaf design can be applied together with another. This will make the overall design appear proper and balanced. For example, the *Kelindu* Fern Curve (m) does not blend well with other curves, with the exception of the curve that appears almost similar to itself, for example, the *Lemiding* Fern Curve (a), the Bowing Curve (g) and the Interlocking Curve (i). The *Bunga Tapang Bubut* Curve (w) is normally beautifully matched by the *Kubok* Fern Outright Bend (x) or with the *Semunjing* Curve (t).

Let us now move on to the jorquette. The jorquette pattern holds a similar importance in the overall design and should be given proper attention, too. The leaves of the designs always overlap, entwine and interlock with the others as shown thus:

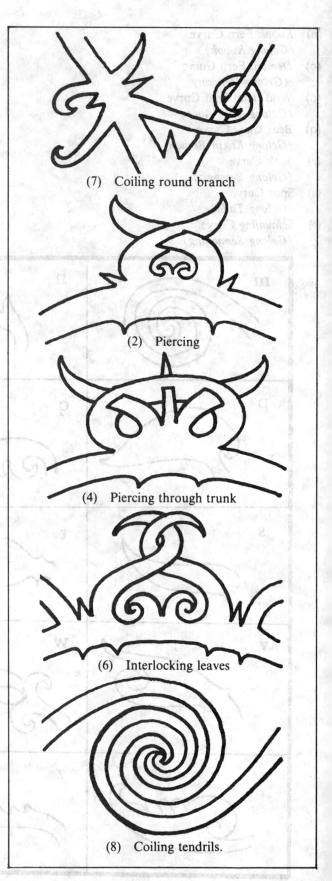

(7) Coiling round branch

(2) Piercing

(4) Piercing through trunk

(6) Interlocking leaves

(8) Coiling tendrils.

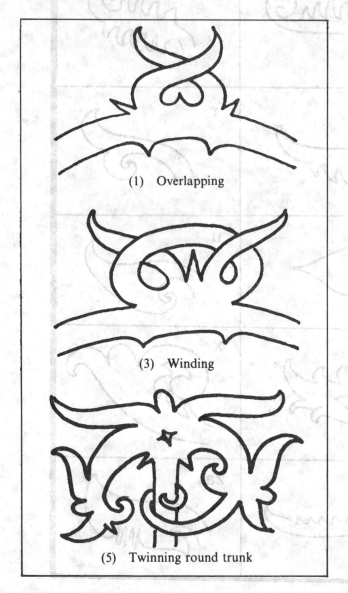

(1) Overlapping

(3) Winding

(5) Twinning round trunk

The jorquette pattern in Figure 4 (a) shows six different kinds of leaves that have been merged to become one jorquette. Leaf (a) appears similar to leaf (b) except for the different directions of their tips. Leaf (a) swings to the left while leaf (b) swings to the right. The same also applies to leaf (c) with leaf (d), and leaf (e) with leaf (f).

THE JORQUETTE

When designing the jorquette attention must also be given to the pattern appearing on the right side. If the leaf on the left side is made from the Bowing Curve (*Gelong Nundok*), then that appearing on the right must be that of the Bowing Curve design, too. If the leaf on the left is of the Bowing Curve, and that on the right is of the Wild Betel Leaf Curve, or other curves, then the jorquette will definitely appear unbalanced. (Figure 4 (b)).

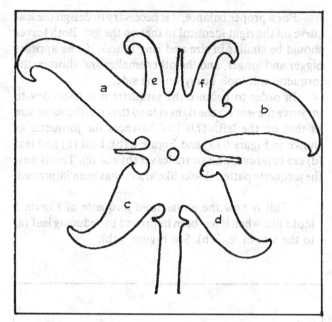

Figure 4　(a) Well-balanced jorquette

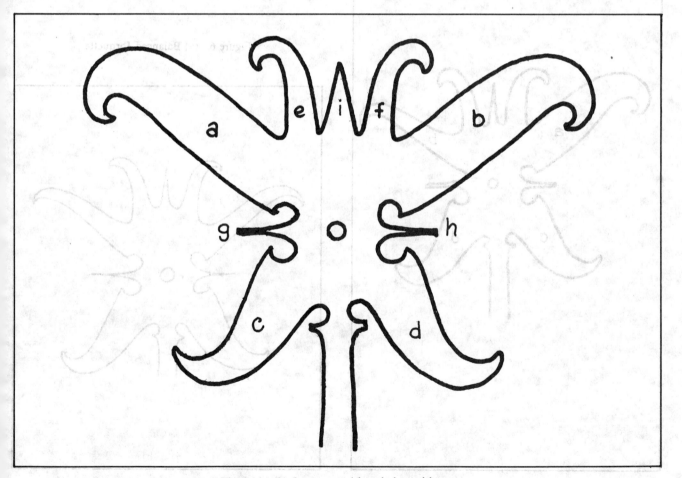

Figure 4　(b) Jorquette with unbalanced leaves

For a proper balance, it is necessary to design the leaf curve on the right identical to that on the left. Both leaves should be similar in size and length, too. If one appears bigger and longer, and the other smaller and shorter, the jorquette will look heavy on one side.

In order to balance the jorquette it is necessary to improve the leaf on the right side so that it is the same size as that on the left. This leaf balances the jorquette as shown in Figure 6 (a) and Figure 6 (b). Leaf (a) and leaf (d) are balanced, and so are leaves (b) and (c). This is how the jorquette pattern looks like after it has been improved.

This is how the unbalanced jorquette of Figure 5 looks like when it has been improved by reducing leaf (a) to the size of leaf (b). See Figure 6 (b).

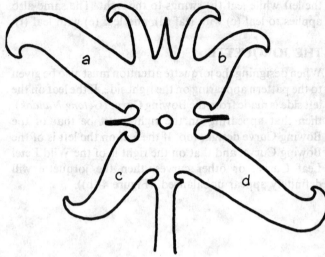

Figure 6   (a) Balanced Jorquette

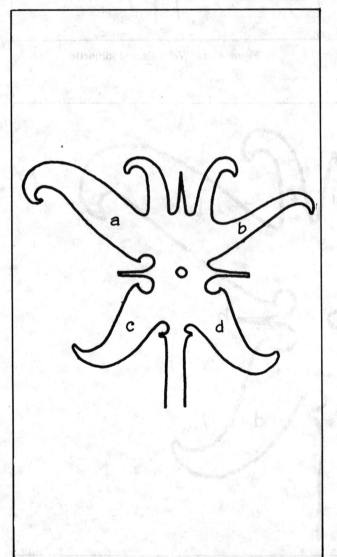

Figure 5   Jorquette showing the leaf heavier on one side.

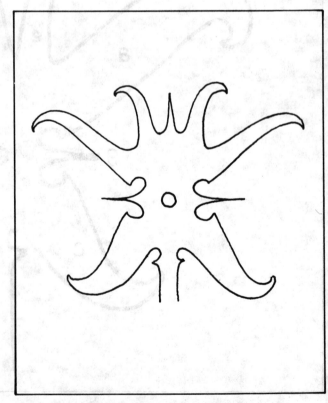

Figure 6   (b) Improved Jorquette of Figure 5.

30

CHUNGGIT

Apart from leaf patterns, another pattern which appears small but extremely useful is the *chunggit* tip.

	Sharp *(Juring)*
	Dibble Stick Tipp *(Lancham Tugal)*
	Rounded *(Dudul)*
	Prawn's Feeler *(Janggut Udang)*
	Butterfly's tongue *(Dilah Kebumbu)*
	Spear Head *(Sangkoh)*
	Semunjing **Fruit** *(Buah Semunjing)*

The chunggit is shaped like a thorn and grows between the leaf and the branch patterns. It comprises seven varieties. One variety is short and pointed, one resembling the tip of a dibble stick, contrasted by a rounded type. Then there are those that are shaped like the prawn's feeler, *simunjing* fruit, a spear head and the butterfly's 'tongue'. Without the *chunggit,* the overall design will not appear complete.

The *chunggit* varieties which are commonly used in designs are the pointed *chunggit* and the Prawn's Feeler *chunggit*. The *Semunjing chunggit* and the Spear *chunggit* are normally used too, but the Dibble Stick Tip *chunggit* and the Butterfly's Tongue *chunggit* are seldom applied. You can only observe this variety on the *Kelingai* designs.

The methods of applying the Semunjing chunggit and the Spear chunggit.

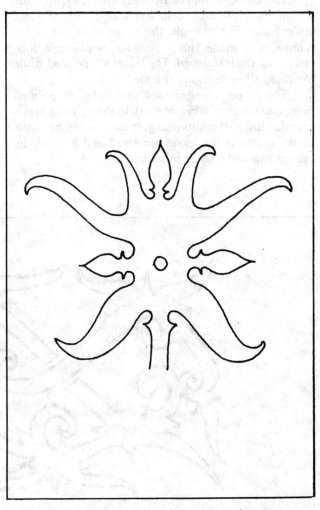

Figure 7   Jorquette with *Semunjing chunggit.*

The two pictures on page 32, i.e., 8 (a) and 8 (b) depict designs with and without the *chunggit.*

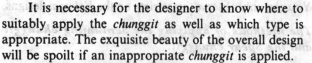

Figure 8   (a) With *chunggit*.

Figure 8   (b) Without *chunggit*.

It is necessary for the designer to know where to suitably apply the *chunggit* as well as which type is appropriate. The exquisite beauty of the overall design will be spoilt if an inappropriate *chunggit* is applied.

The *chunggit* applied depends on the type of the design made. It must also harmonise with the leaf designs used. For example, the design shown i.e., 9 (a), is improperly made. This is because its *chunggit* does not match the leaf design. The leaves are pointed while the *chunggit* patterns are rounded.

The proper *chunggit* used should be the pointed *chunggit* as shown in Figure 9 (b). In short, if one uses a rounded leaf pattern, its *chunggit*, too, should be of the same variety. If the leaves are small and pointed, its *chunggit* should also be small and pointed.

Figure 9 (a) The *chunggit* pattern that is unsuitable.

Figure 9   (b) The suitable *chunggit* pattern.

The portion that is known as *chunggit* in diagram **4** (a) page 29 is cunggit (g), (h) and (i). *Chunggit* (g) and (h) are similar. *Chunggit* (i), though in different form, is in harmony with the rest of the design. As seen in Figure 10 (a) the design can be elaborated further by applying either the *Semunjing* or Spear Head *chunggit*. *Chunggit* (i) may be extended above, with leaves added both to the left and right side, subsequently emerging as a jorquette (Figure 10 (b). None the sprouting *chunggit* as pointed by an arrow. It has been developed and formed into a smaller jorquette. Fig. 10 (b).

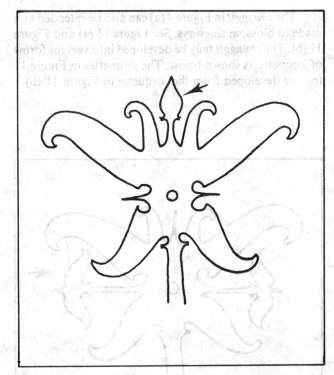

Figure 10 (a)   The jorquette with the *Semunjing chunggit*.

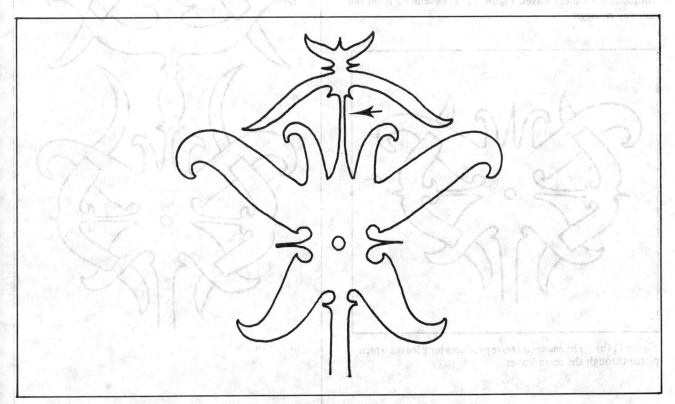

Figure 10 (b) This *Chunggit* is extended to form another jorquette above.

The *chunggit* in Figure 4 (a) can also be extended and made to blossom sideways. See Figure 11 (a) and Figure 11 (b). The *chunggit* may be developed into various forms of jorquette as shown below. The jorquettes in Figure 11 (c), are developed from the jorquette in Figure 11 (b).

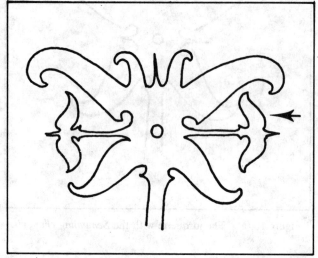

Jorquette with short leaves, Figure 11 (a) developed from the sideway *chunggit*.

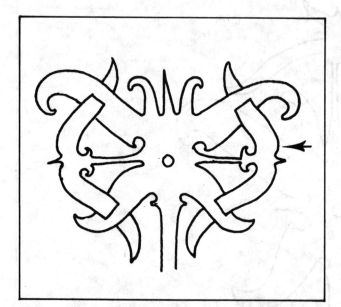

Figure 11 (b)   The *chunggit* above produces long leaves which pierce through the main leaves.

Figure 11 (c)

THE JORQUETTES

There are various ways of making the jorquettes as shown in illustrations 1 to 36 below.

No. 1

No. 2

No. 3

No. 4

No. 5

No. 6

No. 7

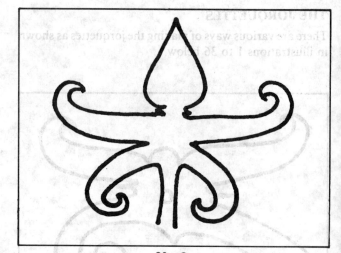

No. 8

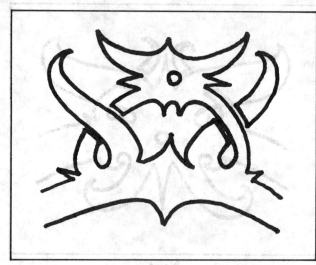

No. 9

No. 10

No. 11

No. 12

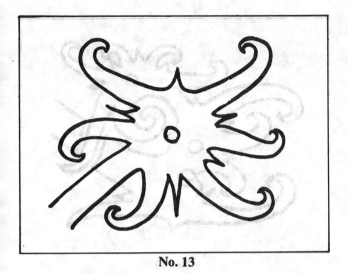

No. 13

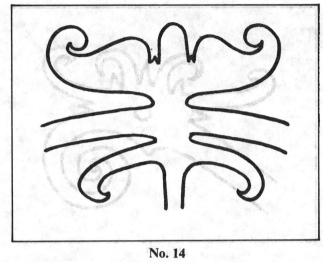

No. 14

No. 15

No. 16

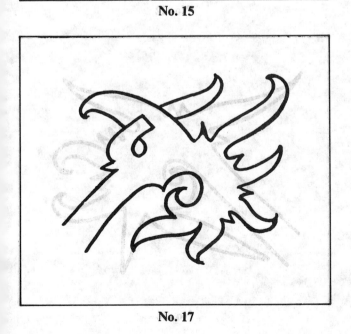

No. 17

No. 18

No. 19

No. 20

No. 21

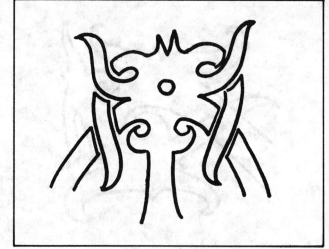

No. 22

No. 23

No. 24

No. 25

No. 26

No. 27

No. 28

No. 29

No. 30

No. 31

No. 32

No. 33

No. 34

No. 35

No. 36

VARIOUS WAYS OF MERGING THE JORQUETTES

Another point that requires close observation in designing is the merging of the jorquettes. If the jorquettes are not merged there appears a separation, which makes the design less attractive, as shown in Figure 12 (a). Notice the contrast with Figure 12 (b), where the jorquettes are merged.

Figure 12 (a)   Separate jorquettes.

Figure 12 (b)   Jorquettes which are merged together.

INNER PATTERNS

We have already touched on the methods of making the *chunggit* patterns rather thoroughly. Let us now deal with the methods of making the Inner Patterns.

The Inner Patterns are patterns within the designs, i.e. the patterns appearing on the leaves, the trunk and the base. Please see Figure 13 (a).

Next to the *chunggit,* the Inner Patterns are of secondary importance. According to tradition, Iban designs have been handed down from generation to generation over an extremely long period. Owing to the ravages of time, the styles of designing have altered, too. In classic Iban designs, the Inner Patterns are always definitely made on the leaf and the leech designs, but the choice of curves, patterns or designs applied rests entirely with the designer himself.

Fig. 13 (a)

The suggested patterns are as follows:

(a)   The Zigzag Pattern.
(b)   The Fish Scale Pattern.
(c)   The Chevron Pattern.
(d)   Zigzag and Chevron Patterns.
(e)   The Triangle Pattern.
(f)   The New Moon Pattern.
(g)   The Semi-Circle Pattern.
(h)   The Semi-Circle with the Chevron Patterns.
(i)   The Diamond Shape Pattern.
(j)   The Criss-Cross Lines Pattern.
(k)   The Ladder Pattern.

(a)   The Zigzag Pattern is quite simple. It only requires drawing lines up and down repeatedly. The Zigzag Pattern can be made more attractive if the designs are accompanied by straight lines drawn on both sides, parallel to the double Zigzag Pattern. See Figure 13

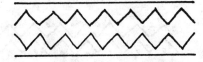

Figure 13 (b)/1
Double Zigzag Pattern with straight lines made on both sides.

The pattern can be further improved by adding the Triangle and the Diamond Shape Patterns. See Figure 13 (b)/2.

Figure 13 (b)/2
Double Zigzag Pattern with straight lines applied on both sides with Triangle and Diamond Shape Patterns added in.

(b) The Fish Scale Pattern.

Figure 13 (b)/3
A Simple Fish Scale Pattern

Figure 13 (b)/4
A Fish Scale Pattern that has been improved.

(c) The Chevron Pattern.

Figure 13 (c)/1
A simple Chevron Pattern.

Figure 13 (c)/2
A Chevron Pattern that has been improved.

(d)   The Zigzag and Chevron Patterns.

Figure 13 (c)/3
A simple Zigzag Pattern and the Chevron Pattern.

43

(e) The Triangle Pattern.

Figure 13 (c)/4
A simple Triangle Pattern.

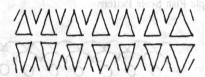

Figure 13 (c)/5
A Triangle Pattern that has been improved, with the addition of a Chevron Pattern.

(f) The New Moon Pattern.

Figure 13 (c)/6
A simple New Moon Pattern.

(g) A Semi-Circle Pattern.

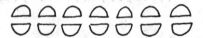

Figure 13 (c)/7
A simple Semi-Circle Pattern.

(h) A Semi-Circle with Chevron Patterns.

Figure 13 (c)/8
A simple Semi-Circle with Chevron Patterns.

(i) The Diamond Shape Pattern.

Figure 13 (d)/1
A simple Diamond Shape Pattern.

Figure 13 (d)/2
A Diamond Shape Pattern that has been improved.

The application of the Inner Patterns (as mentioned above) can be rather difficult on smaller designs. However, the Zigzag Patterns with dots are highly recommended. Examples are:

or

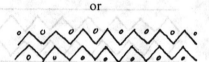

The simplest pattern to apply is the Criss-Cross Lines Pattern. Please see Figure 13 (d)/3.

Figure 13 (d)/3
A simple Criss-Cross Lines Pattern.

Among the various patterns, the Ladder Pattern and the Dot Pattern are the easiest to apply, despite their limited sizes.

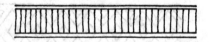

Figure 13 (d)/4
A simple Ladder Pattern.

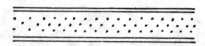

Figure 13 (d)/5
A simple Dot Pattern.

44

Entadu Betangkup

EYE DESIGNS

According to legends, the practice of making designs with eyes was handed down from designer to designer over a long period of time. This shall continue to be perpetuated as long as Dayak designs exist. The application of eyes on design is extremely important because many Dayak designs are derived from animal or giant forms. At first glance, the eyes may look simple and easy to design, but to execute them correctly and attractively is not as simple as they appear to be. If the types of eye pattern applied are wrongly selected, the beauty of the overall design would be affected. It is difficult to explain precisely the type of eye suitable for each kind of design. Each eye should be located at its correct place without disturbing the pattern of that particular design. Listed below are the various types of eye patterns commonly seen on Dayak designs.

The first four types shown below are commonly applied on designs representing human, giant, dragon, bird and animal forms. The four types on the right are commonly made on body tattoo designs. Eye patterns actually help to beautify designs if they harmonise with the overall arrangement of the designs.

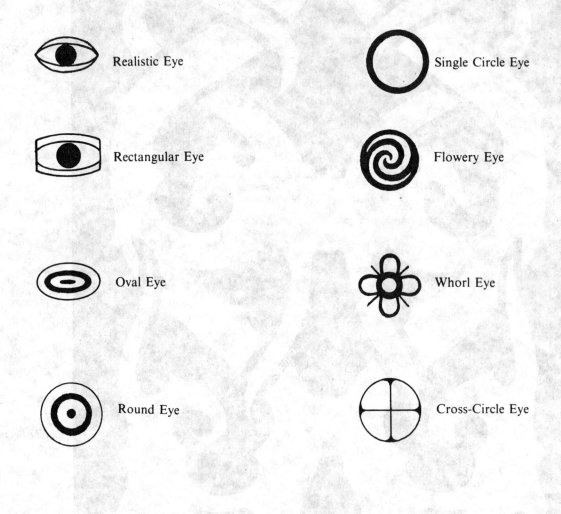

Realistic Eye

Single Circle Eye

Rectangular Eye

Flowery Eye

Oval Eye

Whorl Eye

Round Eye

Cross-Circle Eye

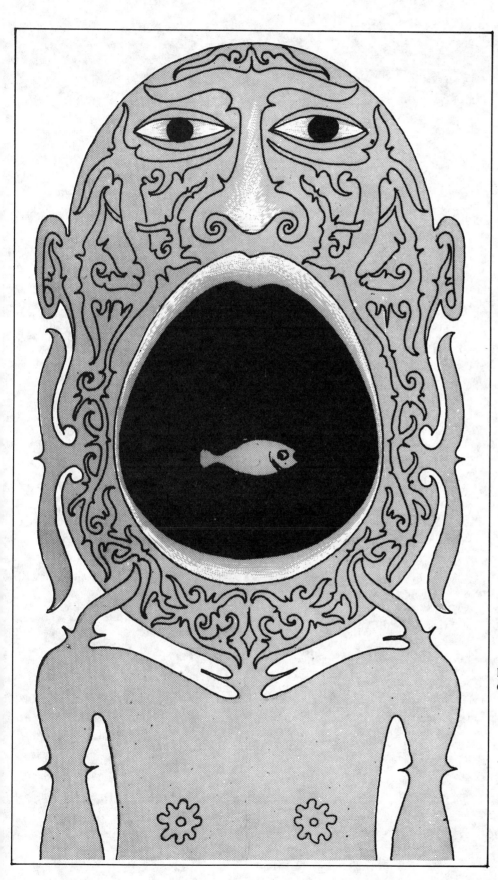

In this design, realistic
eyes are preferable.

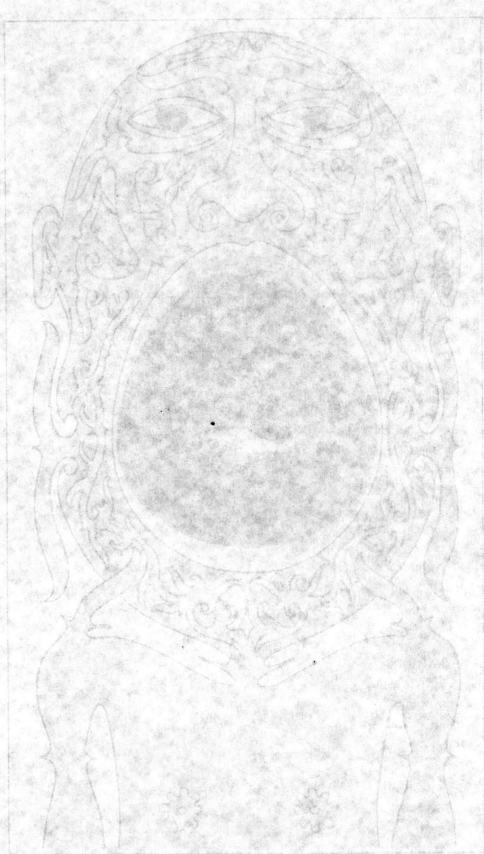

CHAPTER 3

FIVE TYPES OF CURVE

IF we observe a particular design closely, we find that it consists of a trunk or base lines of its own. The work of disigning and beginning a design can be considered difficult because we tend to be doubtful of what should be considered or done initially.

Consideration must first be given regarding the various curves to be utilised. The trunk or base line of designs comprises numerous varieties of curve, but the curves most commonly used can be narrowed down to five types.

Before starting a design, we must consider the types of curve most fitting for the design that is going to be made, and how best these could be arranged so that they could be easily elaborated to become a fine piece of work. If the curves utilised do not fit with the intended design, we will encounter difficulties in executing the design. However, if the arrangement is correct, there would be a feeling that the designing work can be both simple and pleasurable.

The methods of arranging and elaborating the curves are explained step by step. For the benefit of beginner-designers, the methods chosen have been simplified to follow easily. Only basically essential curves are chosen. These are the five types of curve all potential designers should know:-

1. – 'J' curve

2. – 'C' curve

3. – 'V' curve

4. – 'W' curve

5. – 'S' curve

An arrangement of the five types of curve.

51

Let us study the "J" curve first. This particular curve can be arranged and elaborated in various ways.

A. ARRANGEMENT AND ELABORATION OF THE 'J' CURVE

Fig. 1: The first 'J' Curve arrangement and its first elaboration.

Fig. 2: The first 'J' Curve arrangement and its second elaboration.

Fig. 3: The first 'J' Curve arrangment and its third elaboration.

Fig. 4: The second arrangement of the 'J' Curve.

Fig. 5: The third arrangement of the 'J' Curve.

Fig. 6: The fourth 'J' Curve arrangement and its first elaboration.

Fig. 7: The fourth 'J' Curve arrangement and its second elaboration.

Fig. 8: The fourth 'J' Curve arrangement and its third elaboration.

Fig. 9: The fifth 'J' Curve arrangement.

B. ARRANGEMENT AND ELABORATION OF THE 'C' CURVE

The arrangement of 'C' Curve, too, can be arranged and elaborated in different ways:

Fig. 10: The 'C' Curve arrangement and its first elaboration.

Fig. 11: The second arrangement of 'C' Curve.

Fig. 12: The third arrangement of 'C' Curve.

Fig. 13: The fourth arrangement of 'C' Curve.

Fig. 14: The fifth arrangement of 'C' Curve.

Fig. 15: The sixth arrangement of 'C' Curve.

Fig. 16: The seventh arrangement of 'C' Curve.

Fig. 17: The eighth arrangement of 'C' Curve.

Fig. 18: The ninth arrangement of 'C' Curve.

Fig. 19: The tenth arrangement of 'C' Curve.

Fig. 20: The 'C' Curve for the Eleventh Arrangement.

This curve can be arranged as desired, depending on the ability of the designer. It may be arranged downward or crossing to the right. It can also be arranged around a circle in the centre. On the right is illustrated the methods of designing the curve.

C. THE 'V' CURVE ARRANGEMENT

This Curve can be arranged and elaborated in different ways:

Fig. 21: The first 'V' Curve arrangement.

Fig. 22: The second 'V' Curve arrangement.

Fig. 23: The third 'V' Curve arrangement.

Fig. 24: The fourth 'V' Curve arrangement.

Fig. 25: The fifth 'V' Curve arrangement.

Fig. 26: The sixth 'V' Curve arrangement.

Fig. 27: The seventh 'V' Curve arrangement.

Fig. 28: The eight 'V' Curve arrangement.

Fig. 29: The ninth 'V' Curve arrangement.

Fig. 30: The tenth 'V' Curve arrangement.

Fig. 31: The eleventh 'V' Curve arrangement.

D. THE 'W' CURVE ARRANGEMENT

This Curve may also be arranged and elaborated in different ways:

Fig. 32: The first 'W' Curve arrangement.

Fig. 33: The second 'W' Curve arrangement.

Fig. 34: The third 'W' Curve arrangement.

Fig. 35: The fourth 'W' Curve arrangement.

Fig. 36: The fifth 'W' Curve arrangement. (a)

Fig. 37: The fifth 'W' Curve arrangement. (b)

Fig. 38: The sixth 'W' Curve arrangement.

Fig. 39: The seventh 'W' Curve arrangement.

Fig. 40: The eight 'W' Curve arrangement.

E. CURVE 'S' ARRANGEMENT

This Curve is commonly used as the trunk of design and may be arranged and elaborated as follows:

Fig. 41: The first 'S' Curve arrangement.

Fig. 42: The second 'S' Curve arrangement.

Fig. 43: The third 'S' Curve arrangement.

Fig. 44: The fourth 'S' Curve arrangement.

Fig. 45: The fifth 'S' Curve arrangement.

Fig. 46: The sixth 'S' Curve arrangement.

Fig. 47: The seventh 'S' Curve arrangement.

This Curve may be arranged in a circle. The flower of the *terung* fruit may be positioned in the centre, too. However, this flower does not make up the main essence of the design.

F. THE 'J' AND 'V' CURVES

Designs may also begin with two varieties of curves that are connected with each other. Commencing on page 112 are illustrated methods of merging two types of the curve:

Fig. 48: The first 'J' and 'V' Curves arrangement.

Fig. 49: The second 'J' and 'V' Curves arrangement.

Fig. 50: The third 'J' and 'V' Curves arrangement.

G. THE 'V' AND 'C' CURVES

Fig. 51: The first 'V' and 'C' Curves arrangement.

Fig. 52: The second 'V' and 'C' Curves arrangement.

Fig. 53: H. THE ARRANGEMENT OF THE 'W' AND 'C' CURVES

I. THE ARRANGEMENT OF THE 'J' AND 'C' CURVES

Fig. 54: The first 'J' and 'C' Curves arrangement.

Fig. 55: The second 'J' and 'C' Curves arrangement.

Fig. 56: The third 'J' and 'C' Curves arrangement. (a)

Fig. 57: The third 'J' and 'C' Curves arrangement. (b)

Fig. 58: Here are five types of curve arranged together in a simple form.

Figure 1

Figure 2

Figure 3

Figure 4

Figure 5

Figure 6

Figure 7

Figure 8

Figure 9

Figure 10

Figure 11

Figure 12

Figure 13

Figure 14

Figure 15

Figure 16

Figure 17

Figure 18

Figure 19

Figure 20

Figure 21

Figure 22

Figure 23

Figure 24

Figure 25

Figure 26

Figure 27

Figure 28

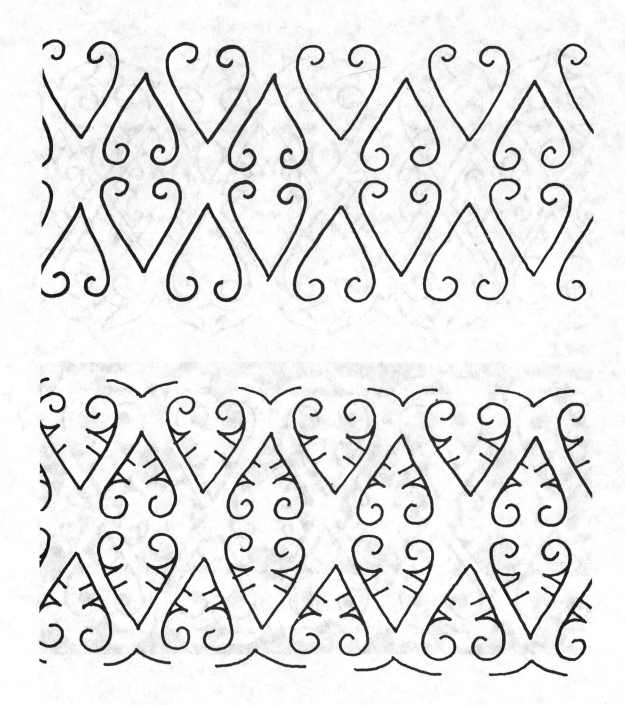

Figure 29

Figure 30

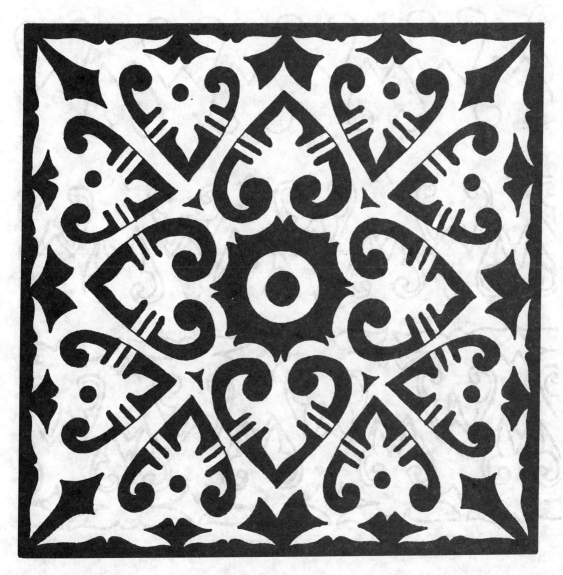

Figure 31

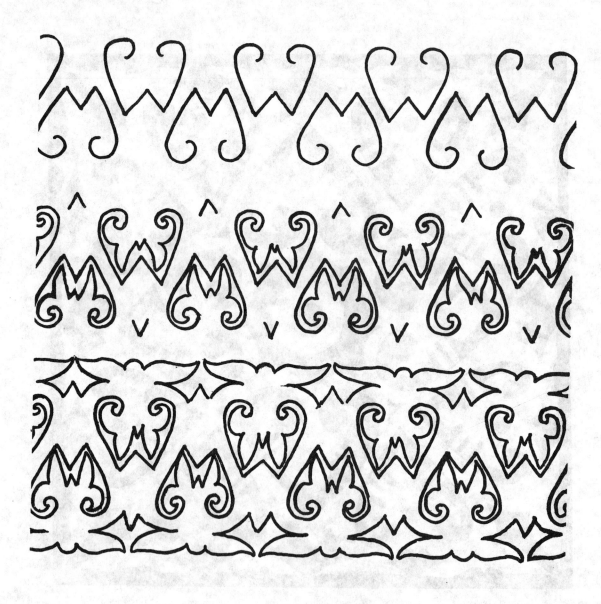

Figure 32

Figure 33

Figure 34

Figure 35

Figure 36

Figure 37

Figure 38

Figure 39

Figure 40

Figure 41

Figure 42

Figure 43

Figure 44

(Continued on next page)

Figure 45

(Continued from page 99)

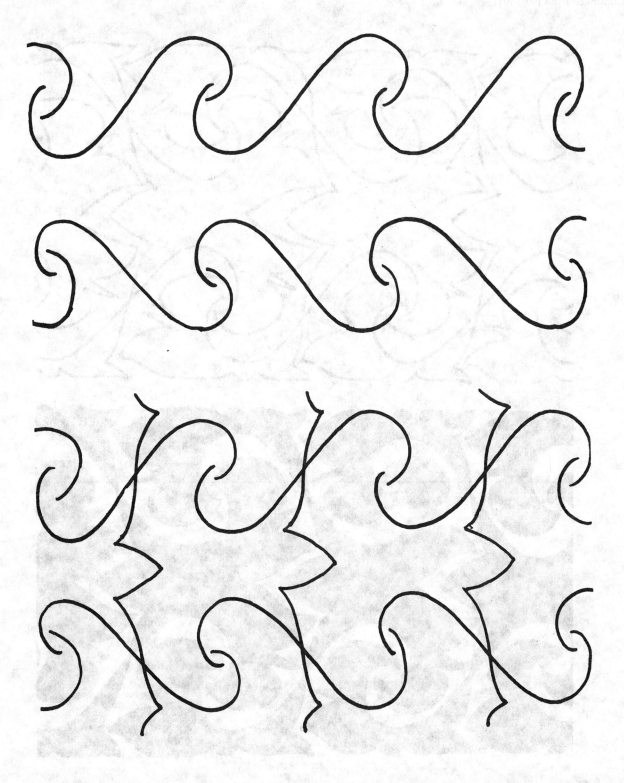

Figure 46

(Continued on next page)

(Continued from page 101)

Figure 47

Figure 48

Figure 49

Figure 50

Figure 51

Figure 52

Figure 53

Figure 54

Figure 55

Figure 56

(Continued on next page)

Figure 57

(Continued from page 113)

Figure 58

THE MERGENCE OF CURVES

Designs may begin with a type of curve that has been merged of joined with other types. In the following designs can be seen the mergence of two types of curve.

Designs may also be made into a pair so that they will appear as one design. This particular design cannot begin with the various types of curve as described before. This design originates from the form of a type of wild dog known as *pasun*. The leaves of this design are of varied sizes, some are long while some are short.

Design: *'Pasun Nyalak Di Lebak Tanah Emperan Pasun Tunggal Ngigal Ngaki Kerangan'*.

116

Design: *Jagu Bekaul Iko*.

Design: *'Antu Rangka'*.

Design: *Entadu Berasok*.

Design: *'Sandah Ngua'*.

CHAPTER 4

TENDRIL DESIGNS

THE designs done by the Kenyah or Kayan tribe bears semblance to Iban designs. Most of their designs appear in tendril forms. It is so called because the curves found in the designs resemble plant tendrils.

This design may have branches in any part of the overall design. It may be rendered big or small, and long or short, according to the space available for executing the design. Normally this design originates from human form or the forms of a human head, animals, mythical dragon, the hornbill bird or even from a circle.

Figure 1: Iban type of tendril designs.

Figure 2: The Iban type of tendril design is quite similar to the tattoo design except that it is more complex.

The Kayan/Kenyah tendrils design is attractive especially because of its varied colours, and its compact and composite designs. Designs encompassing animal, bird and snake forms are realistically arranged to beautify its overall appearance. Notice how the various tendril patterns creep and coil in the design. Shown below are designs of Kenyah/Kayan origin seen in the Sarawak Museum. Observe the varied animal patterns applied in the generally complex tendril designs.

Figure 3: Tendril designs originating from a tree form, in a design called 'The Tree of Life'.

Figure 4: Another 'Tree of Life' design.

Figure 5:
This tendril is developed from the form of a mythical dragon. Notice its protruding tongue, scaly feet and long pointed teeth.

Figure 6:
Another dragon design.

Figure 7:
A Kayan/Kenyah decorative wood carving. It is done on the model of a coffin (lungun) for an aristocrat.

Both designs are of Kayan/Kenyah origin. The tendril design in Fig. 8 depicts a tree with leaves and fruits, and a monkey facing a tiger.

In Fig. 9 the monkey, bird and snake are living in harmony.

Figure 8

Figure 9

Figure 10: A design originating from the form
of a human head.

The development of a form of tendril design.

Another form of tendril design. The steps are shown below.

This one originates form a dog form.

This design, based on a dragon form.

A dragon tendril design.

This design is based on a hornbill form.

This one begins from circles.

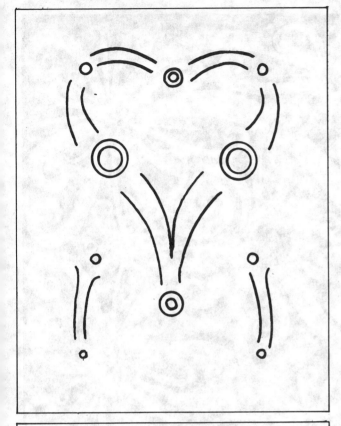

This design originates from the curve that is shown in
Chapter 3, and arranged thus:

A tendril design originates from a tree.

CHAPTER 5

KELINGAI

FORMERLY the Ibans are fond of tattooing their bodies with the Kelingai design. If a male did not tattoo his body, he was regarded as effeminate and cowardly.

The main material used for blackening the tattoo is a type of soot called *along*, with potions from various types of charm added. Those who leave their particular district will normally tattoo the *Kelingai* on their bodies upon reaching a certain place or country. This will serve to symbolise that they have visited the place concerned.

The *Kelingai* design done on the back of the hand and fingers ia called *Entegulun*. The *Entegulun* design cannot be made at one's whim and fancy. It may only be done on the hands of those who have slain or cut off the heads of their enemies.

The *Kelingai* comprises different types of design. Almost all of them can begin with the curves as explained in Chapter 3.

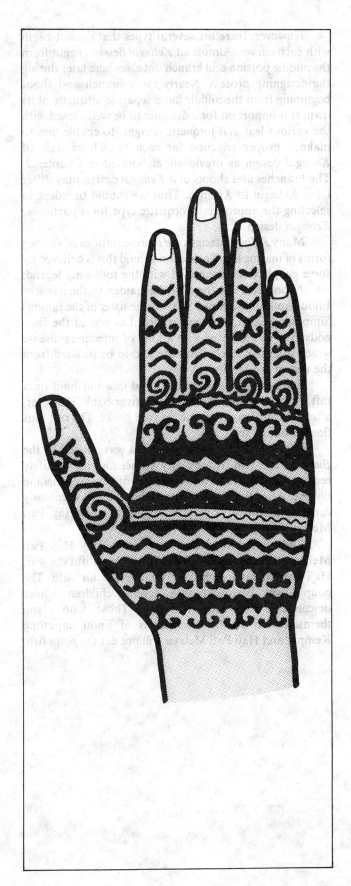

However, there are several types that cannot begin with such curves. Almost all *Kelingai* designs begin from the middle portion and branch out elsewhere later during the designing process. Nearly every branch and shoot beginning from the middle has a separate jorquette of its own. It is important for a designer to be well-versed with the various leaf and jorquette designs, to enable him to make a proper selection for each branch or base of *Kelingai* design as previously elaborated in Chapter 2. The branches and shoots of a *Kelingai* design may differ from *Kelingai* to *Kelingai*. Thus we should be adept in selecting the appropriate jorquette type for a particular *Kelingai* design.

Many *Kelingai* designs are representations of various forms of marine life. The reason behind this is believed by some people to be connected with the following legend:

A long time ago there lived a maiden by the name of Endu Saputong Kempat. She was the sister of the famous Simpulang Gana, who was regarded as one of the Iban gods. She was afflicted with a kind of infectious disease which offensive smell. Thus she had to be isolated from the rest of the family.

Endu Saputong Kempat stayed in a hut built on a raft. A rope secured the raft to the river bank. However, after a certain length of time the rope broke. The raft thus floated out to sea.

Endu Saputong Kempat's plight was noticed by the *Bungsu Patin* fish. It took pity on her and immediately rendered assistance. It also cured her of her foul-smelling disease. After floating for some time, the raft eventually came to a stop at a jetty belonging to one, Haji Pati Melayu.

Endu Saputong Kempat was invited by Haji Pati Melayu to his house. Upon seeing how beautiful she was, Haji Pati Melayu immediately made her his wife. The couple was bestowed with several children whose descendants last until this day. Those who claim themselves to be the descendants of Endu Saputong Kempat and Haji Pati Melayu will not eat the *patin* fish.

The *Patin* fish talking to Endu Seputong Kempat and curing her
of her infectious disease.

The close association of certain Ibans with the sea resulted in the adoption of marine life forms in some on their *Kelingai* designs. These forms comprises prawns, crabs, and sea horses. Some designs may be greatly elaborated to make them appear more interesting. They may be modified according to each designer's skill. The more competent a designer is, the more exquisite the designs will be.

Figure 1: A Malay design which is quite similar to the Iban leaf design in Chapter 8.

Figure 2: A Kenyah design. Dragon forms are usually found in Kayan and Kenyah designs.

Marine life designs. On the left are drawing showing actual marine life forms, while on the right are the modified drawings forming the *Kelingai* designs.

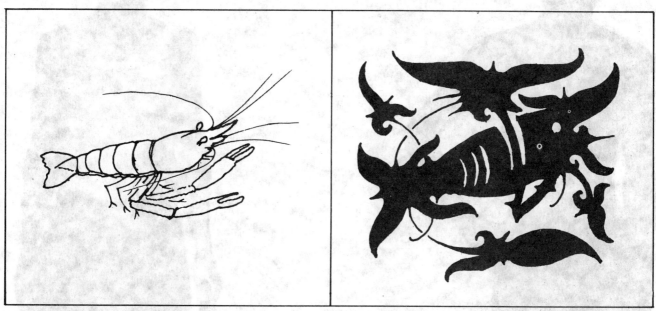

Figure 3(a): Prawn

Figure 3(b): *Undai Beredai*

Figure 4(a): Crab

Figure 4(b): *Ketam nyepit*

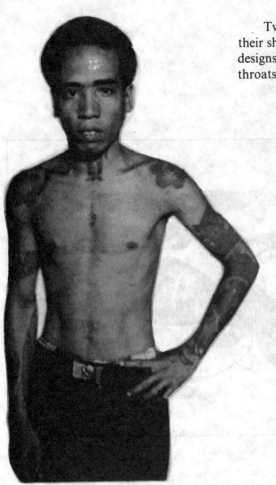

Two tattooed gentlemen. On their shoulders are Brinjal Flower designs, while those found on their throats are Scorpion designs.

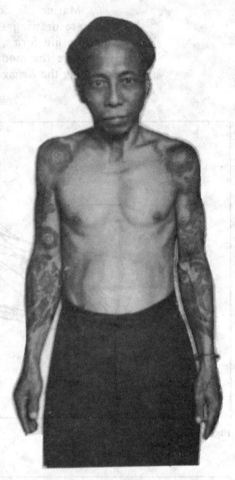

Figure 5

Let us observe carefully how a *Kelingai* is being designed. It is known as the *Ketam Bedayung* (Rowing Crab) design. The design starts from the 'C' Curve. The final result can be seen on page 148.

[a]

[b]

Figure 6: *Ketam Bedayung Kelingai*. The final result of 'C' Curve arrangement.

Kelingai Gerama Murong. This *Kelingai* starts with 'C' & 'S' Curves. The final result can be seen on page 149.

Figure 7: *Kelingai Gerama Murong* – Final result of the 'C' and 'S' Curves arrangement.

Here are the methods of begining and elaborating a *Kelingai* originating from a circle, then merging with the curves. Notice how the curves of the overall design interlock, merge with and oppose each other.

Figure 8

150

This *Kelingai* begins with an eight-sided shape and reinforced by the 'V' Curve and straight lines. Bottom right is a final elaboration of this *Kelingai* design.

'V' curve and straight-lines.

Bottom right is a final elaboration of this Kelingai design.

Figure 9

This *Kelingai* is known as *Kelingai Tabak*. It begins with the shape of a triangle, and is later joined by 'C', 'J' and 'S' Curves.

Figure 10

This *Kelingai* begins with the shape of a square and
further elaborated with a few curves.

Figure 11

This *Kelingai* begins with a somewhat oblong figure and elaborated with the 'J' and 'C' Curves and straight lines.

Figure 12

The *Kelingai* design below is made up of various patterns. The design itself is called *Kelingai Ajat Pama* (the Dancing Frog Design).

Figure 13

Figure 14

Figure 15: *Kelingai Dulang Sempandai* (The Sempandai God's
Tray Design).

Figure 16: *Ketam Ngerayap* (Crawling Crab).

Figure 17

Figure 18

Figure 19: *Baya Butang* (Adulterous Crocodiles)

Figure 20: *Bunga Terung* (Brinjal Flower)

Figure 21: *Rengguang* (Lobster)

Figure 22: *Pala Rusa* (Deer's Head)

Figure 23: *Tedong Beambai* (Mating Cobra)

Figure 24: *Dulang Ini Manang* (Goddess Ini Manang's
Tray Design).

Figure 25: *Janggut Undai* (Prawn's Feelers)

Figure 26: *Kala Bejagang* (Crawling Scorpion)

Figure 27: *Bekaul Kawai* (Interlock)

Figure 28: *Semawa* (Flying Fox)

Figure 29: *Jelenga Udun* (V-Shape Cut)

Figure 30: *Surong Gelang* (Bracelet)

Figure 31: *Gerasi Papa Saum Nyawa* (Two Giants With
One Mouth)

Iban women tattoo their hands with zigzag patterns. However, for the Kenyah tribe, only the women of high standing can be tattooed. The Kelabit and Kayan women prefer to tattoo their legs.

Both men on the left are amply tattooed with various types of designs.

Shown below are Iban wooden tattoo blocks.

CHAPTER 6

LEECH DESIGNS

MOST Sarawakians have seen the handles of war knives like the *jempul* and other types. If we observe such handles closely we notice that the patterns resemble leeches. Thus the design is known as 'Leech Design'.

The Leech Design is not only used for decorating knife handles. It may also be used for decorating the scabbards. The design may begin anywhere and may also be applied on any suitable area of the object to be decorated. However, an important factor to note is that the overall design must comprise large and small leeches, and the accompanying curves should either be long or short, sharp or blunt and round or pierced. Between the leeches should be executed the base pattern so as to 'bind' the leeches together, and also to act as 'homes' for them.

Shown below are methods explaining the elaboration of the Leech Design. Before following the methods on beginning and elaborating this particular design, we must initially be familiar with the varieties of suitable leech patterns.

Shown below are illustrations of sixteen types of

curve that must be memorised to make it easier for us to elaborate the Leech Design. The curves are easy to execute. The head of a leech may be designed to meet the tail of another, or the tail of the leech may be designed to meet the back of another leech.

Shown below are the methods of arranging the Leech Design so that the leeches on each side are of equal number. For instance, if three leeches are carved on the left, three should also appear on the right side.

The arrangement of this design depends on the shape of the object which is being decorated; whether it be round, square, triangular or oblong. If the object is circular in shape, we may arrange the position of the leeches thus:

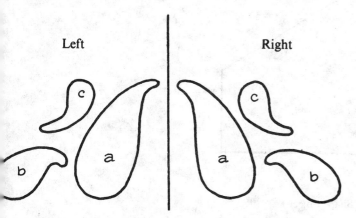

Arranged in accordance with a circular shape.

If leech (a) on the left appears large and long, leech (a) on the right must be of the same size also so that the patterns appear balanced. The same goes for patterns 'a' and 'b' on the left and 'a' and 'b' on the right.

It is suggested that one executes the patterns on the left first before beginning with those on the right. Designs done between the curves of the leeches must be close to the contour of the leeches. See illustration below:

Facing each other

This design may be further elaborated with the Brinjal Flower Design, placed right at the centre of the leech arrangement.

Note that the designs are placed in between the leeches. The inner patterns may also be applied.

171

If the shape of the object that requires designing is similar to that as shown below, we must think of the most appropriate curve to accompany it, and position it at the centre. This would serve as the trunk of the overall design. The general arrangement of the Leech Design can be done later.

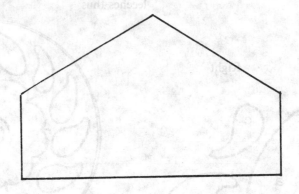

Chevron Shape object.

The arrangement of the leech patterns according to space available.

The completed Leech Design.

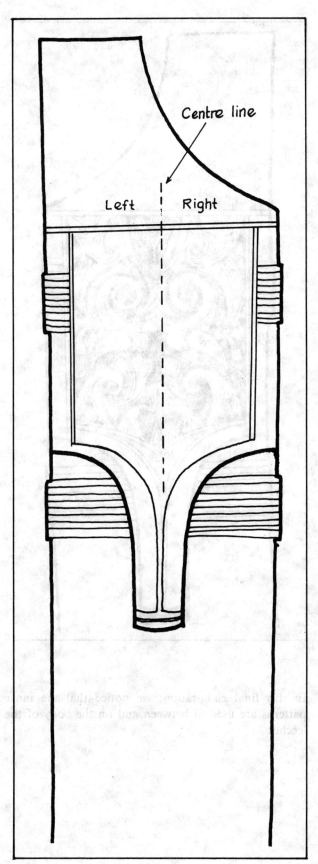

If we have a scabbard of this shape to be decorated with the Leech Design, what sort of leeches or curves should we use? First we should start from the middle and advance gradually to the left and right. We may only put three or four leeches on both sides, then fill the gaps with other pattens. The leeches may interlock or overlap.

The next step is to fill any available space with other patterns. Inner patterns may be applied on the body of the leeches.

This illustration creates an impression that the leeches are piercing through the designs from underneath.

An almost-completed Leech Design on a scabbard.

In this final elaboration, we notice that the inner patterns are used in between and on the body of the leeches.

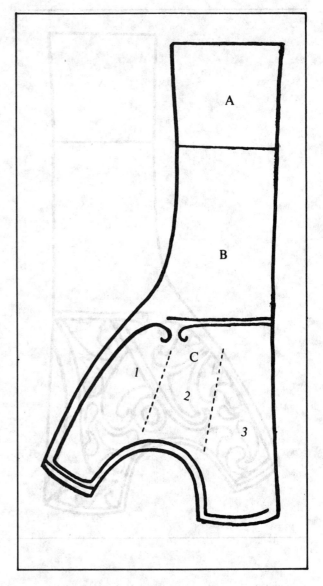

This is the shape of the *jempul* war-knife handle. Such handles are either made of wood or deer horns. To ease the work of designing, the surface of the handle is divided into three sections, based on the sections that have to be designed and also on the particular type of design that best suits the handle.

Section A: For making the *simpai,* a kind of binding so that the handle will not break.

Section B: Left empty.

Section C: The section to be designed.

The section which should be given the fullest attention is Section C. This section should also be sub-divided into three parts to ease designing work. After this, the appropriate patterns should be determined, then executed on Section C (3) of the handle. The circular designs should be inserted right in the middle of section C (2), to act as the 'eyes' of the designs.

Any shape of the leech patterns may be applied on (1) and (3), whether it be long or short, sharp or blunt and so on.

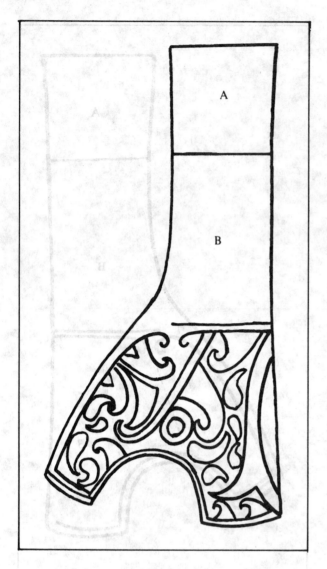

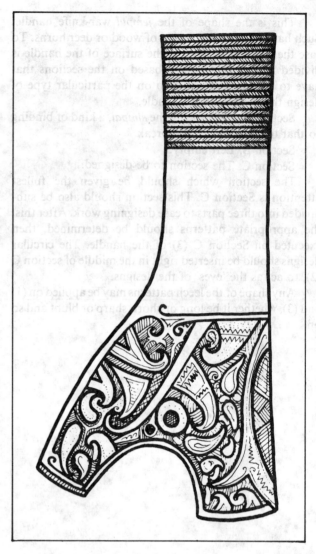

This is the method of carving the Leech Design on to the knife. Notice the leech shapes that have been arranged; some are big, some small, some are long while some are short.

The overall appearance of the knife handle after completion. In Section A, braided wire is used in the *simpai* binding.

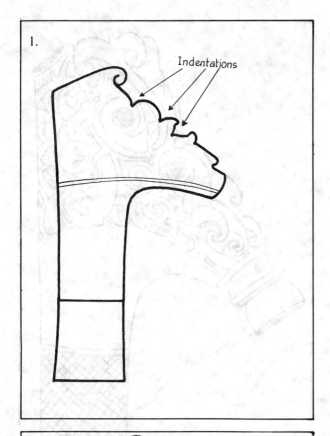

1. This is another type of a war-knife handle. The methods of making the Leech Design here is similar to the one just explained for the *jempul* war-knife handle.
2. The arrangment of the leech patterns on the handle.
3. This is how the completed Leech Design appears.

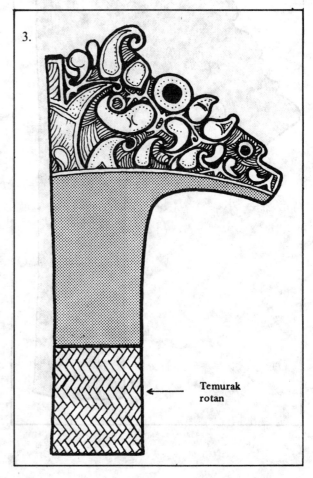

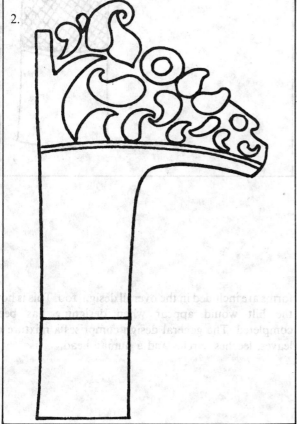

177

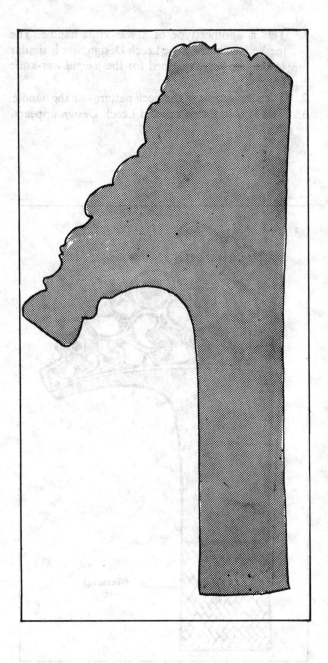 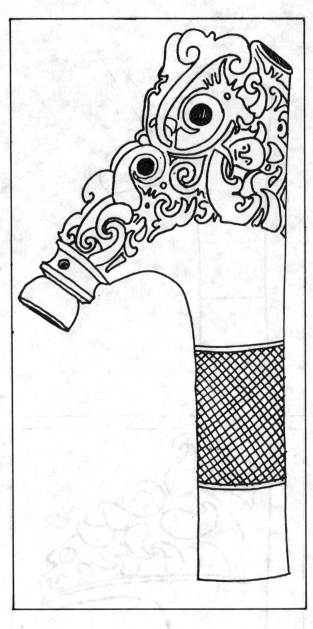

Before we proceed with the general design for the hilt, we should initially begin with the outline. When the actual shape of the hilt has been completed, we can then apply the most appropriate types of design and various leeches on it. Sometimes, birds, animals and human·forms are included in the overall design, too. This is how the hilt would appear when designing has been completed. The general design comprises a mixture of leaves, leeches, circles and a human head.

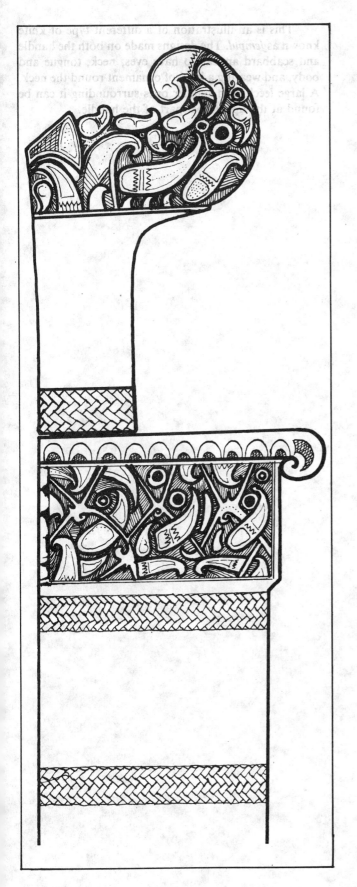

This is an illustration of the handle and the upper part of the scabbard of a *chandong* knife which is decorated with the Leech Design. The knife is short and easy to carry about. Many owners design their *chandong* handles and scabbards with animal, bird and leech patterns.

If we observe the designs in this illustration carefully, we notice that they are not that difficult to make. Using only the leech pattern, a variety of shapes can be created, i.e. long, short, big, small, round, sharp, blunt and so on. Another important factor that must be given due attention here is the inner designs or the patterns applied on the leeches themselves. Without these patterns, the leeches would appear bare and unattractive. Short stripes and concavities are also inserted between the leeches.

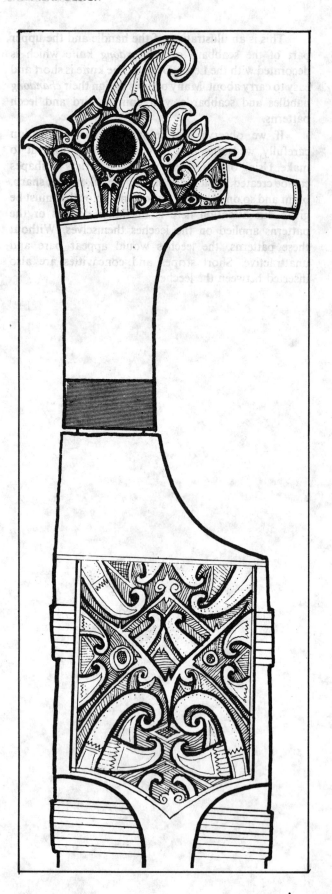

This is an illustration of a different type of knife known as *jempul*. The designs made on both the handle and scabbard appear to have eyes, neck, tongue and body, and wearing a kind of ornament round the neck. A large leech with smaller ones surrounding it can be found at the uppermost part of the handle.

In this illustration we see the effect of the inner patterns on the leeches and on the empty sections between the leeches.

The surface of a table can
also be decorated with incised
or relief Leech Designs.

CHAPTER 7

SHIELD DESIGNS

IN former days, a shield *(terabai)* was essential to an Iban. The *terabai* was used to protect him from the enemy's spear or sword in any combat. Why is a shield decorated with designs? Please read the legend "Lang Ngindang and Lang Kachang" in Chapter 1 of this book.

Some people believed that if the designs found on the shield of an Iban warrior appear more attractive and is of a higher standard in comparison with his enemy's, it is believed that the shield will increase his zest and courage in fighting. However, this again depends on individual luck. There are instances when designs cannot be of assistance. Belief apart, a beautifully-decorated shield is a source of pride to the owner.

It is believed by some Ibans that a warrior's luck may improve by adopting nicknames like *Tedong Ngelantar* (Sliding Cobra) and *Kilat Nyelar* (Striking Lightning). The cobra is a deadly snake, while the lightning is a kind of force that can kill rapidly. Thus *Kilat Nyelar* can be said to be more powerful than *Tedong Ngelantar*. However, *Kilat Nyelar* is inferior to the nickname *Kelambi Kubal* (Rubber Coat), while *Kelambi Kubal* is defeated by *Tedong Ngelantar*.

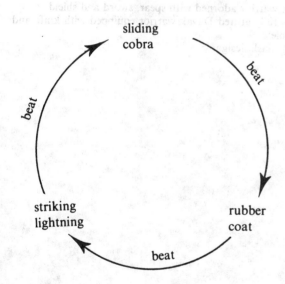

A.

C.

A. A warrior adorned with spear, sword and shield.
B. A fully-attired Dayak warrior equipped with knife and shield.
C. A mask design.

B

Here are the methods of executing designs on a shield. The designs must have the eye and mouth patterns because these form the base patterns. The eye and mouth patterns may be elaborated with curves as shown in Chapter 3. Later, the curves may be created to become the trunk pattern of the designs.

Shield designs begin from 'J', 'W' and 'C' Curves and reinforced by circles and ovals.

189

Shield designs may also begin from similar curves as shown before but in a different arrangement.

Some shield designs do not include the eye and mouth patterns. Some designs are of dragon and hornbill forms. The most common shield designs are the giant and human designs.

Why is a shield made pointed at both its upper and lower ends? The reason is that it is easy to carry it about. In the jungle the shield will not get entangled easily among the bushes when its owner executes his movements. In combat a warrior may be reluctant to strike at his enemy first for fear that his war-knife might get stuck in the enemy's shield. This would make it easier for the enemy to leap and cut him down.

This shield is designed with only one type of curve, i.e. the 'J' Curve. The illustration on the right outlines the methods of arranging and elaborating the curves.

The shield designs on the following page begin from the curves as drawn below:

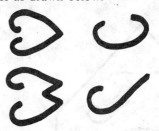

The eyes developed from circular shapes placed inside an elliptic called *Sengkerong Buah Empit*. This is the elliptical shape of the *empit* fruit.

The mouth is an elongated oblong.

    The completed work may look complicated. However, if you observe the arrangement of the curves at Stage 1 carefully, it is not that difficult to create the design.

    The parts that must be dealt with initially are the eye and mouth patterns, followed later by other patterns, utilising the curves as shown above.

STEP 1   STEP 2   STEP 3

This shield design appears rather complicated. However, the curve used is of one type only, the 'J' Curve. The mouth is oblong.

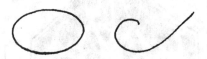

The design is made up of the tendril pattern, which is also known as a Kenyah or Kayan design. Almost all Kenyah or Kayan designs portray tendrils with long pointed leaves, curving at their tips like the *kelindu* fern.

Outline of the design

This shield design began with the various curves as illustrated below.

A point that must be borne in mind when making a design is the method of arranging the various curves. The ways of elaborating them should be fairly simple once the designer has studied all about the jorquettes or the leaf patterns.

Its trunks must merge with or be connected to the others. The ends of the leaves must also be connected to the trunk pattern nearest to it.

The following sheild design begins from only two types of curves, the 'J' and 'C' Curves.

Step 1   Step 2   Step 3

This shield is devoid of the mouth and eye patterns, thus making the designing work easier.

The leaf tip patterns found in this shield neither overlap nor are they connected to the rest except for the pair found at each end, as well as at the top and bottom parts of the design.

Illustration showing the method of doing the design.

STEP 1   STEP 2   STEP 3

This design begins from 'J' and 'C', two circles and an oval shape.
The eyes are based on the shape of a circle, while the mouth is an oblong.

The arrangement begins at the centre of the shield, followed by the eyes and mouth. This is later joined by other curves as found in Stage 1 of this diagram.

| STEP 1 | STEP 2 | STEP 3 |

This shield design begins with two types of curve: The 'J' and 'V' Curves. The additional curve is a mouth curve.

In this design we observe the various positioning of the different patterns used. The pattern in section A is different than the pattern found in section B, while that in section B is also different from the pattern found in section C. However, the patterns harmonise into a design.

Step 1   Step 2   Step 3

STEP 1   STEP 2   STEP 3

199

This shield design comprises three head patterns: one in the middle, one above and one below. The design begins from three types of curve as illustrated.

Although this is the tendril design, it represents an Iban design, not Kayan or Kenyah. The tips of the leaves are not long or pointed. The trunk of the design merges with other designs. This design contains numerous *chunggit* (tips or thorns). It is called the *Pala Antu Gerasi* (Giant's Head) design, but some people call it *Pala Numbing* (Mask Head) design.

Step 1   Step 2   Step 3

STEP 1   STEP 2   STEP 3

The various types of curves used in this shield design are as illustrated below:

The eyes of this design do not begin with circles. They develop from leaf tip patterns as found in section A (Stage 1). The mouth is based on the leaf tip curve design as explained in section B (Stage 1).

The shoots of curves (a) and (b) may not always be of the same length. These shoots may also be designed long or short, depending on the size of the object to be decorated.

Please see Stage 1 in section C.

STEP 1   STEP 2   STEP 3

The 'J' and 'V' Curves patterns are applied on this shield. The eyes are based on the shape of a circle. Sharp tips or thorns *(chunggit)* have been inserted on the left and right eyes.

This design possesses two mouths, one at the bottom section and one above. The structure of the designs made at the lower end is similar to the one at the upper end.

Diagram showing this shield design.

STEP 1   STEP 2   STEP 3

More shield designs.

This is a big replica of a shield, 8 feet high and 5 feet wide. It was used to decorate a stall during a development exhibition in Sibu, Sarawak in 1975. It was decorated with the Kayan-Kenyah tendril design.

The photograph of the shield on page 200. On the right hand side is another type of shield that has a mouth pattern in the middle, a set of eye patterns at the top and another at the bottom.

This shield design from (left) shows the 'Giant's Head' (*Pala Antu Gerasi)* variety. One head is in the middle, one at the bottom while the other can be found at the top. The three heads are connected by some designs in between.

This shield design (left) is typical of the Kayan-Kenyah intricate tendrils. It has one big mouth design at the centre of the design, a set of eye patterns over the mouth, and another set below the mouth.

This is part of a shield design. It begins with the human head pattern and is only given elaboration at the upper part.

A Giant's Barking Dog *Pasun Nyalak*

CHAPTER 8

LEAF DESIGNS

THE Iban Leaf Design is almost similar to the Malay
Floral Design.

Common leaf and jorquette in Iban Leaf Design.

A Malay design.

A dragon carving. It is called *Antu Junan* and is used in various ceremonies.

The famous Iban hornbill carving. Human, animal, bird and plant figures are incorporated.

Another hornbill design is shown below. It is not so complicated. Hornbill images are normally used in a ritual ceremony called *Gawai Kenyalang*, to honour the God of war, *(Sengalang Burung)*. A wooden hornbill image is placed on top of a pole called *chandi*, which is placed at the centre of the platform *(tanju)* belonging to the chief celebrant of the ceremony.

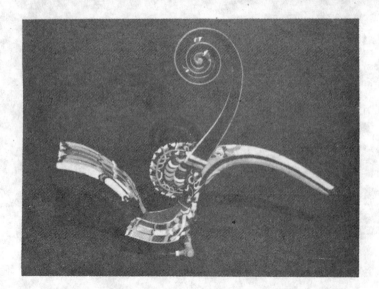

Model of an Iban House For The Dead *(Sungkup)*. It is designed with the *Kelubang* and leaf patterns. A *Sungkup* will last for many years, even after the entire paintwork has become dull.

This leaf design is called *Ejabai nguntai*. Note that each stalk goes up and bends down to form a single round first jorquette and goes up again to form the second jorquette.

The leaf design is not difficult to create if one is familiar with the various leaf patterns that should be used. Shown below are illustrations of leaf patterns normally used.

Once we have familiarised ourselves with the various leaf and floral patterns in this particular design the task of designing is easier. We need to follow the proper arrangement so that the patterns will harmonise.

The method of arranging the leaves in the overall design is similar to that for the tendril design arrangement. We must know where to fill up the voids so that there is always a sense of continuity. For example, if an empty space takes up only a small area, the leaf design applied to that area must also be small. A space that is longish would require a design that is similar in length so that its stem, too, may be contained therein. Usually the *chunggit* may be inserted between the leaves. The more appropriate *chunggit* would be the 'pointed shoots' type or the 'blunt tips or thorns' type.

We are at liberty to arrange the leaves of this particular design according to our preferences. However, it is the normal practice to place them confronting each other or back to back to the nearest pattern.

The ends of the leaves of the pattern on the right curve to the right, while that found on the left curve to the left.

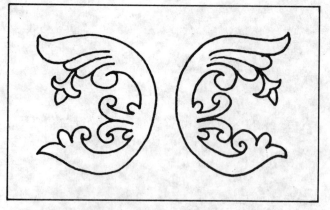

If the leaves of this design are made facing each other, the leaf ends on the left will curve to the right while the ones on the right will curve to the left.

The leaves found on the left and right must be of similar sizes and shapes. The two leaves are balanced, whether they meet face to face, or back to back, and whether they touch the feet or the head of the design.

The leaf patterns are arranged back to back.

Leaf patterns arranged facing each other.

Leaf patterns arranged face to face, and the heads and legs are connected with each other.

216

A flower or a leaf may be inserted right in the centre if desired. This flower or leaf should not resemble that found on the left or right of it. It normally stands isolated.

The leaf or floral shape normally placed at the centre of the design.

The methods of designing or using this isolated flower is fairly easy because it may be placed at the centre of the leaf design. It can be regarded as the base of the design to be made.

Very often these isolated flowers are arranged one after another repeatedly to form a design as shown below.

The leaves forming the leaf design usually contain flowers sprouting from their tips. Occasionally they do become the base of the design. Bud or blooming flower pattern is frequently used. Please see the illustration on the right.

Sometimes the left patterns overlap, pierce, interlace or interlock.

See illustration below.
(a) Overlapping.
(b) Piercing.
(c) Interlacing.
(d) Interlocking.

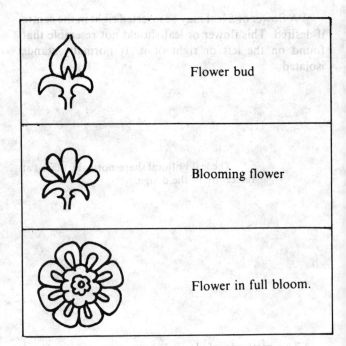

Flower bud

Blooming flower

Flower in full bloom.

Before arranging the leaf design, the trunk or the base design must be done first, to act as guidelines for the design, as illustrated below.

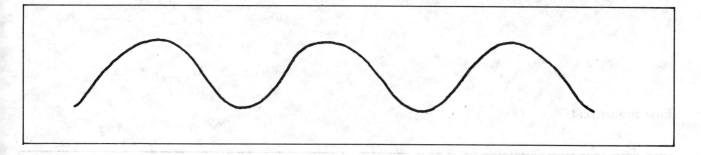

The curves outlined in Chapter 3 may also be used, but only Curve 'J' is utilised frequently. This curve can be arranged as illustrated here, i.e. before the leaf design is applied.

Occasionally the design may be executed directly, without applying the guidelines, as shown below.

Now let us observe the arrangement and method of elaborating this type of design. Remember that the trunk of the design has to be attended to initially before arranging and elaborating the various patterns.

First arrangement.

Second arrangement.

Third arrangement.

Fourth arrangement.

Fifth arrangement.

Sixth arrangement.

Seventh arrangement.

Eighth arrangement.

Ninth arrangement.

Tenth arrangement.

Eleventh arrangement.

Twelfth arrangement.

Thirteenth arrangement.

Fourteenth arrangement.

Fifteenth arrangement.

Sixteenth arrangement.

Seventeenth arrangement.

Eighteenth arrangement.

REVERSE DESIGNS

The design illustrated in (c) below appears complicated and difficult to execute. Actually it consists of two designs that have been merged. The design at the top (a) is similar to that shown below (b). The mergence of (a) and (b) produce (c).

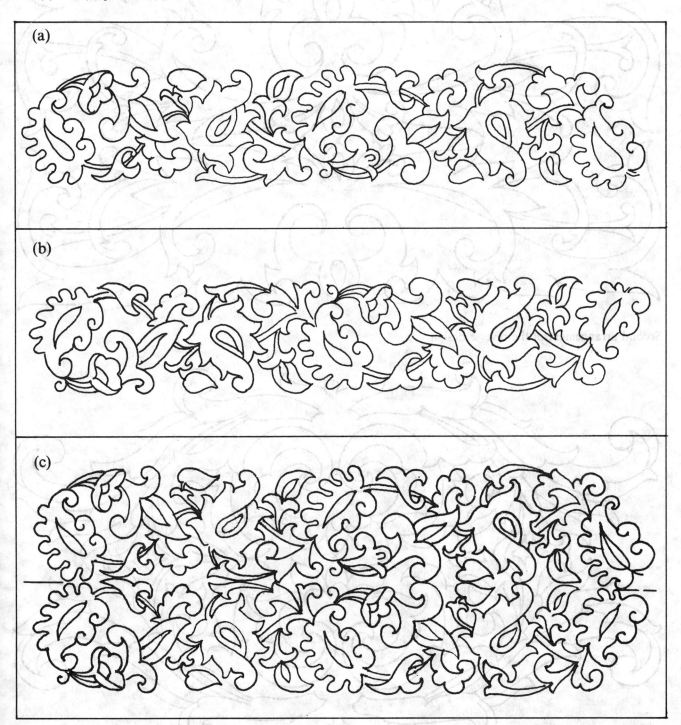

(a)

(b)

(c)

Combination of (a) and (b)

First arrangement of the reverse design.

Second arrangement of the reverse design.

Third arrangement of the reverse design.

Fourth arrangement of the reverse design.

Both have been merged with the *Chunggit Semunjing* and the *Chunggit Dudul* designs.

Fifth arrangement of the reverse design.

Sixth arrangement of the reverse design.

These leaf ends appear balanced. Five leaf blade patterns together with two *Chunggit Juring* and four *Chunggit Dudul* form the designs. The design found on the right (b) is the reverse of the one shown on the left (a).

A whole leaf design is also shown below. It comprises four leaf ends with similar shapes. When combined, these shapes formed the leaf design as shown below. The portion that has been blackened forms the inner patterns of the design.

233

REPETITIVE DESIGNS

The design below is called *dejai*. It has been designed
from the jorquette that can stand side by side. They are
connected by patterns as illustrated by (a) and (b) to
form a design.

Three different types of leaf designs.

These three varieties of design can be drawn from left to right repeatedly until the desired length is achieved.

These designs may also be interspersed as illustrated in Chart A. B is placed beside A, followed by C. Then A again, and so on.

If the arrangement from left to right is alternated, the arrangement below must also be alternated.

Notice the representation of the patterns by alphabets on the right. If the patterns are interspersed, every pattern must be of the same size.

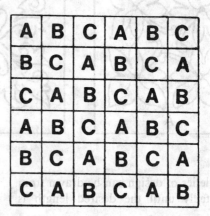

Arrangement table

A suggested ceiling design.

This design can be made on the upper part of a wall, door, bed or settee. The design can either be carved onto or painted on the wood. But the former is preferable as the design would appear in relief form, and rendered more durable.

Note that the design on the right portion is the same as that of the left portion.

The design depicted on the next page is suitable for decorating picture, mirror and door frames.

This design is produced form two similar opposing patterns. The patterns start at the bottom and develop upwards. This design is suitable for decorating ceilings and walls.

Design: *Senggang Beraie*.

The methods of designing depend very much on the shape of the object to be decorated. When designing a rounded object, for instance, the design must be executed in such a way as to make it compatible with the object. The design shown above is called *Besurong Gelang*.

This design begins from the curves as outlined in Chapter 3. They are arranged thus:

Design: *Rajang Merundai*

Design: *Entuyut.* (Pitcher plant)

The *Rajang Segempong* design above began from the centre. Later the branches and leaves developed left and right in equal proportions.

CHAPTER 9

BENT DESIGNS

MAT or basket designs are quite similar in appearance, while those applied on woven cloths are different. A person who weaves a mat should be skilful enough to design the correct number of 'eyes' (points) on the mat. If the 'eyes' are inaccurately done, the overall mat designs will not harmonise.

The type of designs applied on Iban weavings and matwork is called Bent Design. Bent Designs are different from other designs as discussed in this book so far.

Have you ever observed in detail the *pua kumbu,* the woven cloths (*kain tenun*) and the *kain songket* (a type of cloth which is embroidered with gold or silver threads)? The type of designs applied on Iban weavings and matwork is called Bent Design. Bent Designs are different from other designs as discussed in this book so far. In the olden days, before the emergence of commercial cloths in Sarawak, most Iban women in Sarawak knew how to weave cloths. The women's skill varied from person to person. Other then on weaving, this type of design can also be applied on walls and ceilings.

Here we can see that the *Empit* or Rhomb pattern is placed in the middle as a base pattern, and the *Kunchi* or Key patterns are attached to it as branches or leaves.

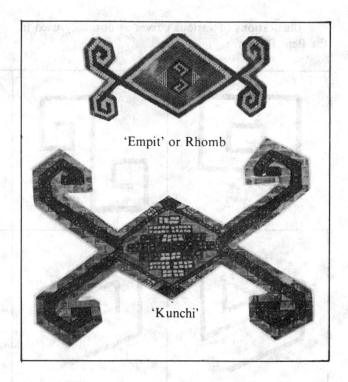

'Empit' or Rhomb

'Kunchi'

Below left:
Bent Design made of multi-coloured beads.

Below right:
Bent Design applied on a woven cloth.

251

Illustrations of various curves as normally used in the Bent Design.

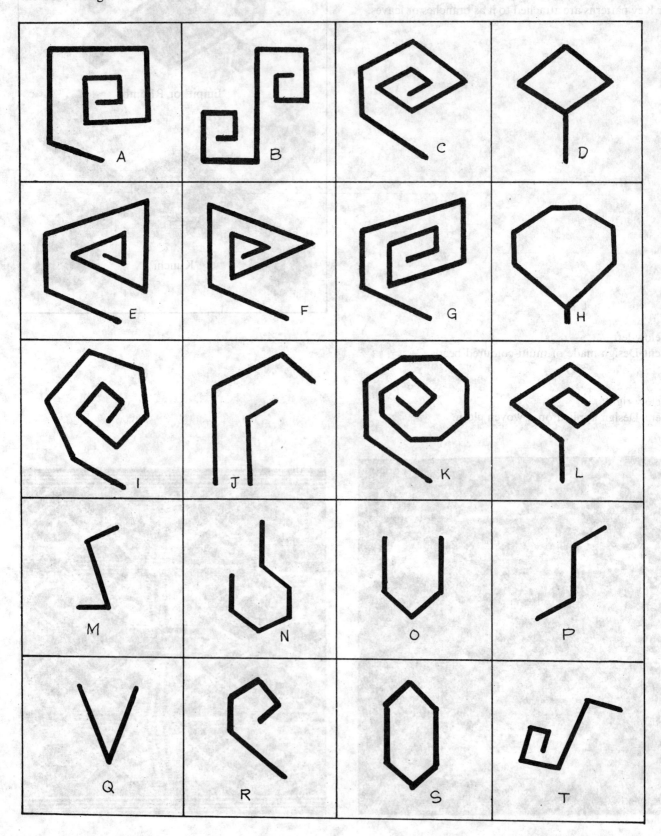

The arrangement of these curves may be done in accordance with individual preference. It may be arranged facing each other, back to back, or joined at the bottom and top sections.

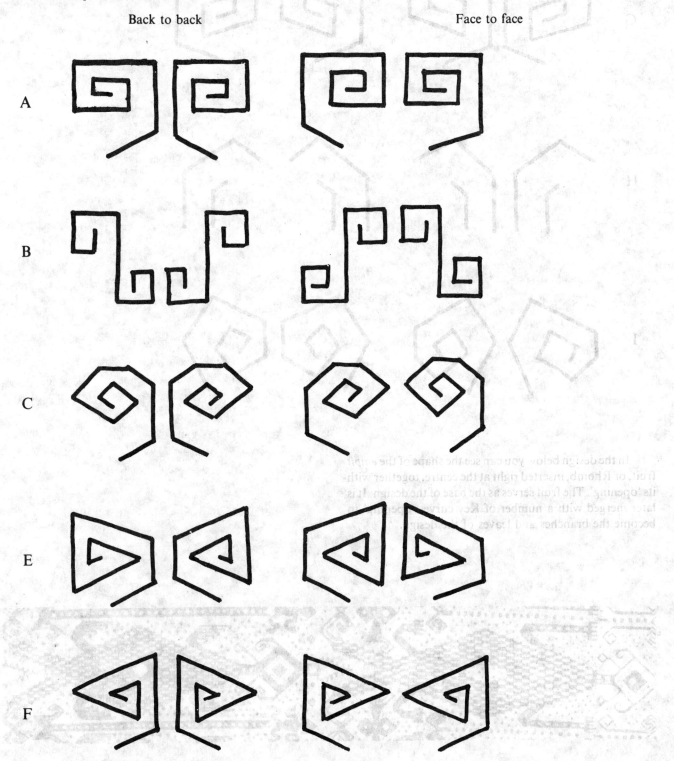

Back to back   Face to face

A

B

C

E

F

In the design below, you can see the shape of the spiral, or Khmb, inserted right at the centre, together with its opening. The front serves as the base of the design. It is later merged with a number of Key curves which become the branches and leaves of the design.

(continued on next page)

G

H

I

In the design below you can see the shape of the *empit* fruit, or Rhomb, inserted right at the centre, together with its 'opening'. The fruit serves as the base of the design. It is later merged with a number of Key curves 'opening' to become the branches and leaves of the design.

Back to back   Face to face

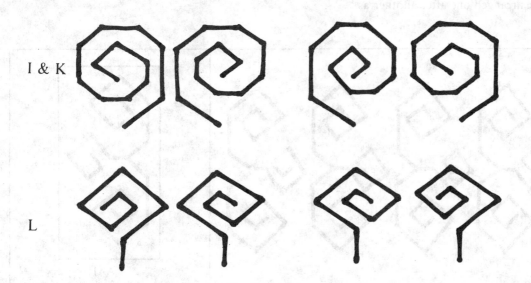

I & K

L

Curves 'D' and 'H' on page 252 cannot be arranged face to face or back to back because they do not have 'faces' or 'backs' like other curves. Curves A, B, C, E, F, G, I, J, K, L can be arranged back to back or face to face. They may also be arranged feet to feet as shown in the illustration. See Curve 'A' on the right.

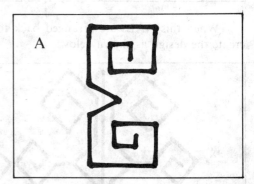

A

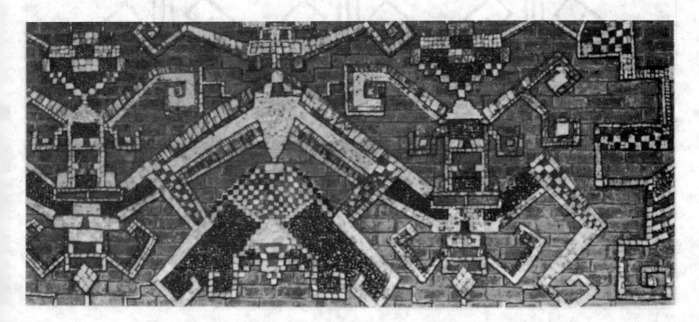

In the illustration below two curves marked 'A' are merged with each other, and Curve 'L' joined at its 'feet'.

Both the curves 'A's and Curve 'L' may be called AAL. This AAL can be arranged one after another as seen below.

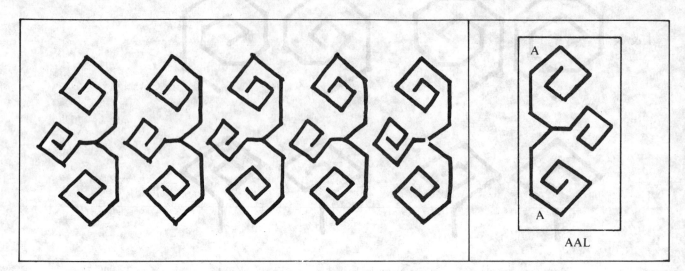

AAL

When this AALs are arranged back to back we create the design as shown below:

Below are Bamboo Shoot patterns arranged one after the other.

Up to this point we have understood something about the curves utilized in the Bent Design. With the exception of the Leech Design, the Bent Design must have its trunk.

From this trunk, the design will produce leaves. Later it splits up into specific sections here and there. We insert the branches in various sections only after its trunk has been completed. The types of curve to be applied depend on the shape of the trunk that has been designed, and also upon the designer's choice.

The steps of arranging, elaborating and completing the design concerned are illustrated below.

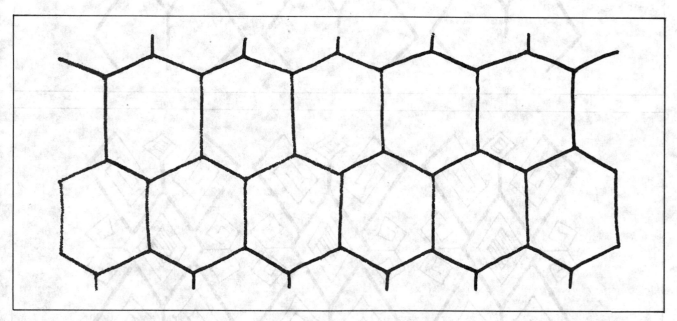

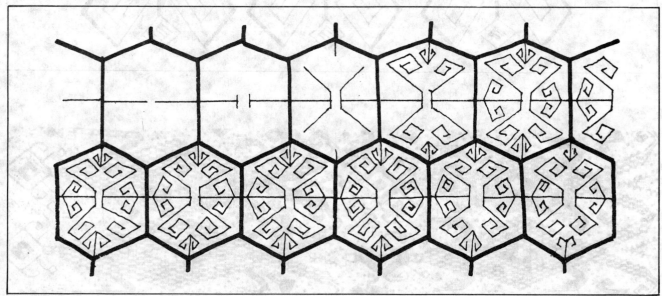

Bent Design developed from the 'empit' or Rhomb form.

Bent Design developed from Curves L, M, N and O.

    Curves H as Head
    Curves MM as Body
    Curves NN as Feet
    Curves OO as Hand

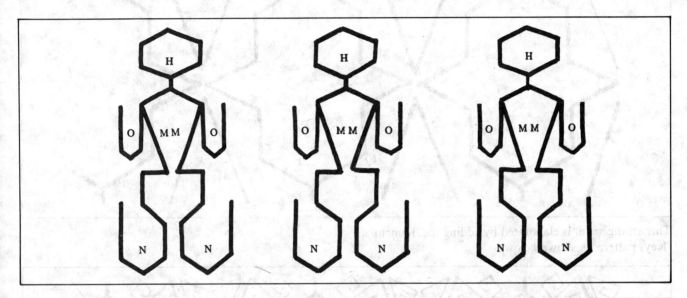

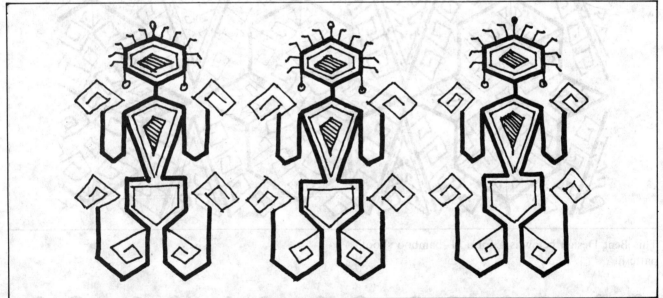

Bent Design developed from P and Q curves. They are arranged as shown below.

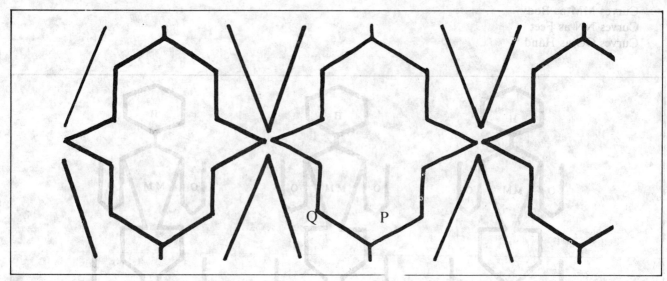

This arrangement is elaborated by adding the 'Kunchi' (Key) pattern as shown below.

This Bent Design below is a form of 'bamboo shoot' pattern.

Bent Design which has been developed from the H and
Q curves.

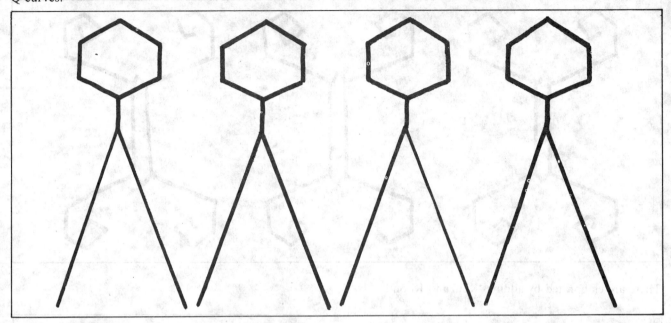

The above designs are elaborated by adding 'Key'
curves.

This one begins from the R and S curves.

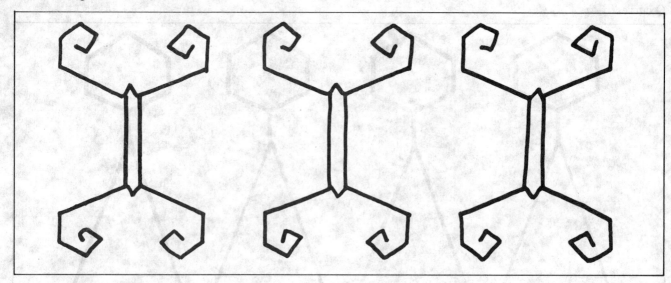

These are elaborated by adding 'Key' and Rhombs.

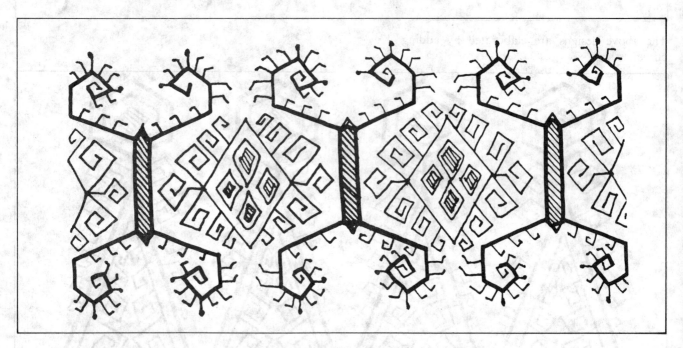

This Bent Design begins from R, J, P and T curves and elaborated simply by adding 'Key' curves and a few Rhombs.

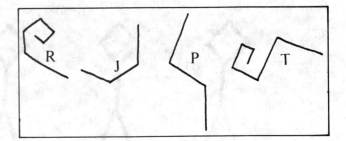

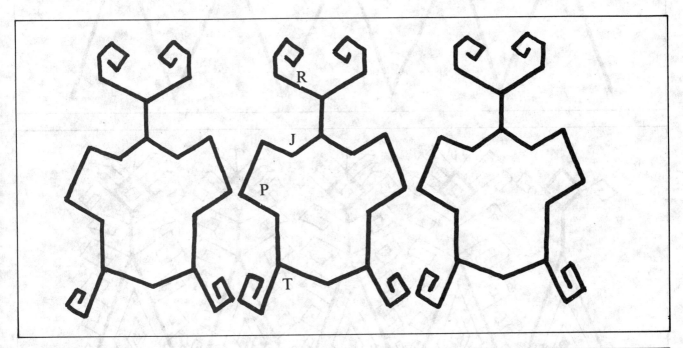

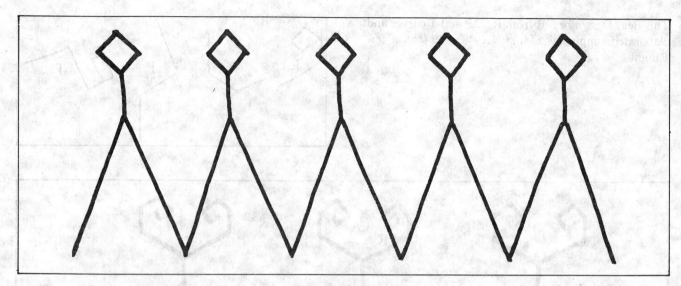

The design above begins from the D and Q curves.

The *pua* weaving pattern shown above is called *Kera Rakang*. There are two types of monkeys *(Kera)* in this design. One has a long body, long legs and a long tail while the other has a short body and tail and 'ringkai' flower on its head.

The *pua* pattern shown below is called *Kamba Nangong*. The decorationg on its head is similar to that found on the head of the *Rakang* monkey. This *Kamba* is short and tailless.

265

This design is called *Menyeti Bali Betangkai*. It is utilised as patterns for the Iban *pua kumbu* weaving. Under careful scrutiny designs (A) and (B) appear similar and well-balanced. When (A) and (B) are merged we see how well-balanced the design is; it does not look heavy on one side.

This *pua* weaving design is called *Bunsu Rabing Mangah Gayau Bedayung* (Fierce Spirit of the Crocodile). The crocodile figures have been woven in lines side by side. Should the *pua* be of a bigger and longer piece, more crocodiles would have to be included. The voids between the crocodiles are normally filled with smaller designs or dots only, or even fish and frog shapes.

A type of *pua kumbu*.

A kain pandak skirt pattern.

Another type of *pua kumbu* pattern

A *pua kumbu*

It is necessary to state here that the 'Rhomb' and 'Key' patterns are usually incorporated in many of the *pua kumbu* designs. The beadwork designs of the handicrafts shown below show some applications of the 'Rhomb' and 'Key' patterns.

A

B

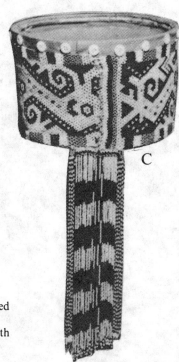

C

A – A basket decorated with designs made with coloured beads.
B – A basket for carrying an infant, decorated with colourful beads.
C – Another decorative beadwork.

It is necessary to say here that the Khans used

ornaments usually incorporated in many of the

pots Anghus designs. The bends in a basket of the

handicrafts shown below show some arrangement in the

Baourie and Kwa ... tribe.

A – A basket decorated with beadwork made with coloured
beads.

B – A basket for carrying an infant, decorated with
colourful beads.

Another decorative beadwork.

CHAPTER 10

BORDER DESIGNS

BORDER Design is not really significant in designing. However, it should be studied for an additional knowledge on designs. Such a design is found also in the bard's *(lemambang)* ritual chanting board and stick. Border Design consists of supplementary patterns for isolating one design from the other, hence its name. There are many types of Border Design, and the choice is normaly left to individual preference. Some illustration of the designs are given here as guidelines for designers.

An example of the application of Border Design on a bamboo tube. Although the additional patterns are not that important, they are able to enhance the beauty of the overall design. The Iban *pua kumbu* weaving and mat, for instance, usually contain Border Designs.

Here are various examples of the Border Design.

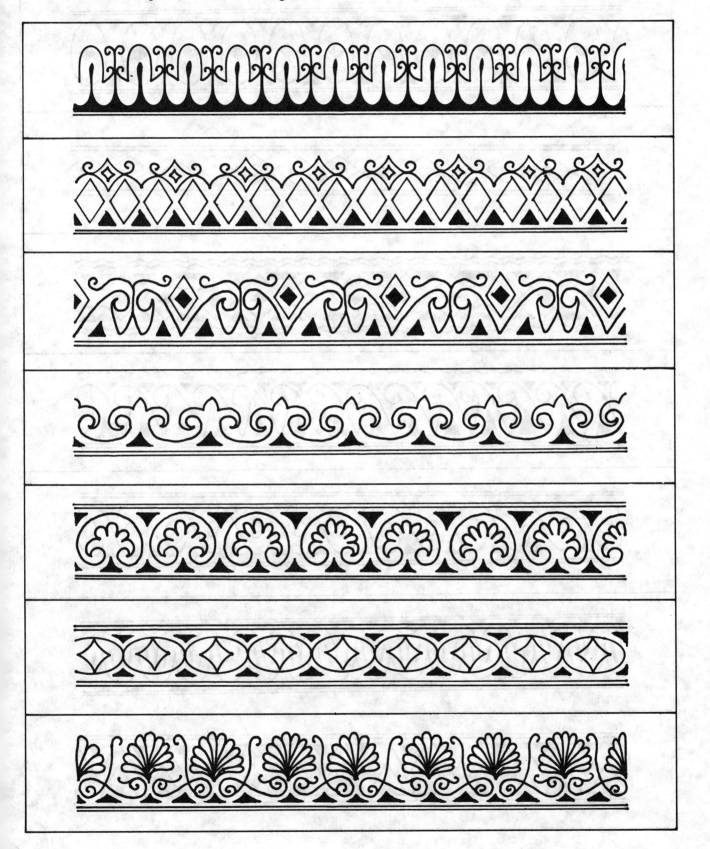

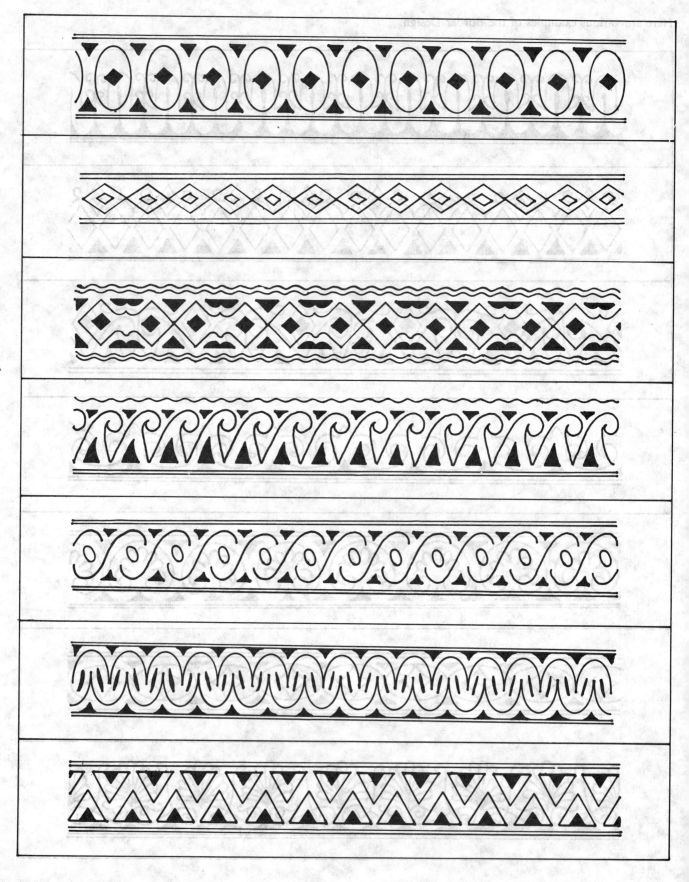

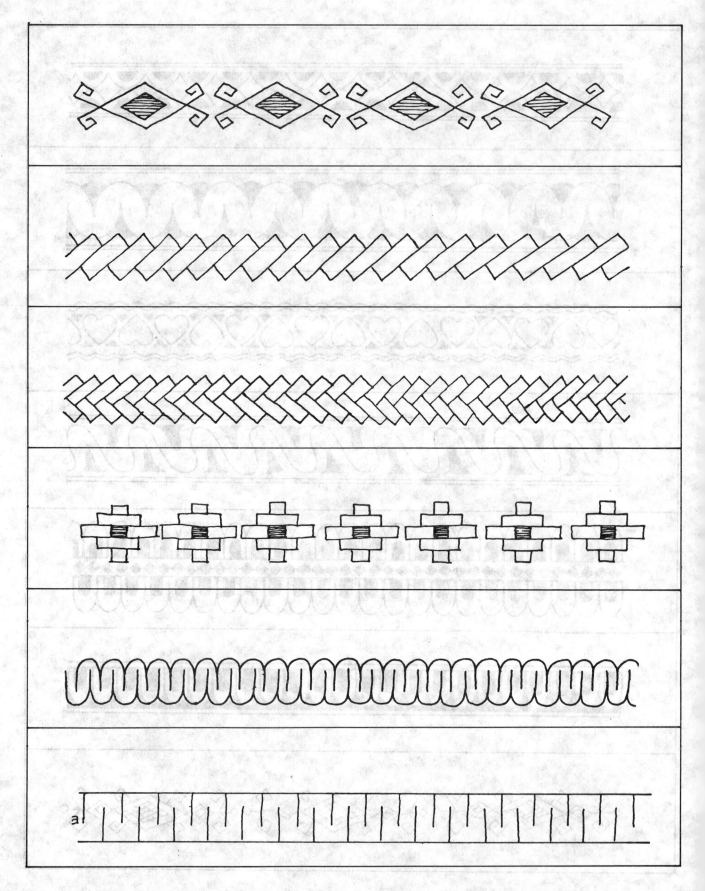

The small and large dwarf patterns.

The lizard patterns.

The bee patterns.

The *empit* fruit and dented 'Key' patterns.

The bamboo shoot patterns.

281

This is a type of sun-hat used by Iban women. Various Border Designs are applied on this sun-hat. Two obvious ones are the wavy design and the 'eyes' of the *punai* bird. In fact, the 'eyes' of the *punai* can be arranged one after the other repeatedly to form a Border Design. This is shown in the middle of the *empit* fruit (Rhombs) and 'Keys'.

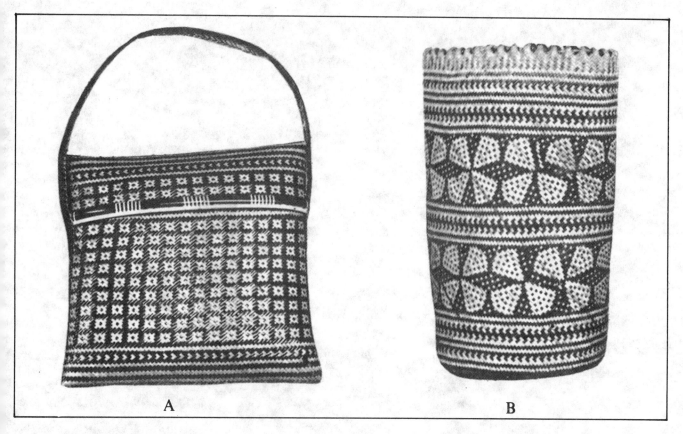

A

B

In basket 'A' above the order patterns are placed in rows. The chevron designs are produced repeatedly. The floral patterns form the main designs.

Basket 'B' is decorated with the *punai* bird's eye patterns.

Shown below are illustrations of Border Design based on insect forms.

An insect Border Design.

Another insect Border Design.

CHAPTER 11

THE USES OF DESIGNS

Almost every society has its own traditional designs, which are executed and appreciated in their respective peculiar ways. Two societies may be neighbours, yet their designs may be different from each other's. For example, the Ibans and Kenyahs are both natives of Sarawak, yet their designs differ.

The Moaris of New Zealand have designs of their own, too. Their designs bear slight similarities to Kenyah designs. The Moaris' appreciation of designs have grown to the extent of having designs applied on their faces and thighs. The posts of their houses are also decorated with designs.

On the right is a *Jerunai* or *Kelideng* burial pole.

A Moari design.

The Red Indian tribes also possess designs of their own. Their designs do not utilise curves, these are mostly circles, triangles and lines only.

Some people regard that if a house does not bear any design it looks vacant. However, if it contains too much of it, the beauty will be spoilt.

Some Red Indian designs comprise the employment of some of these patterns.

Wall designs can be executed in mosaic form also. This is the Batu Lintang Teachers' Training College's Library, Kuching. The designs on the wall are done with coloured pebbles.

If a wall is made of wood it may be designed by using the relief method. A coat of varnish is normally applied over the part that has been designed. Designs may also be painted with coloured paints.

Designs are also made along the upper part of the wall separating the family room and the main gallery of an Iban longhouse. The designs normally begin on the door and are later elaborated to the left and to the right portions of the wall.

An arch in the Batu Lintang Teachers' Training College, Kuching. The designs were done by trainee teachers and the author of this book in 1966. It was designed by using incised method panels.

A leaf design. The design begins from the upper portion of the door, later elaborated to the left and right parts of the wall.

Another wall design.

Apart from walls, the ceiling may also be decorated with designs. Designing is a difficult task if the ceiling boards have already been fitted. The designs should be made beforehand.

Ceiling designs are different from wall designs. This is because ceiling boards are often in sections. The general shape of the ceiling designs depends very much on the position of the ceiling. The designs may differ from section to section. However, the general appearance of the designs should harmonise.

Identical ceiling designs.

Varied designs.

The top part of a post may appear attractive when decorated with designs. The post to be designed need not necessarily be that of concrete only; designs may also be made on a wooden post. Designs are also made on the posts of school buildings, community halls, churches, arches and other public structures.

The top part of the pillars of the Kuching General Post Office building.

292

The arch at the Batu Lintang Teachers'
Training College, Kuching, Sarawak.

Design made on an arch erected during a
festival in Marudi, Sarawak, in 1975.

In olden days the corpse of a Melanau aristocrat was usually stored in a jar and later placed at the top of a belian post which was decorated with designs. The post is called *Jerunai* or *Kelideng*. The *Kelideng* shown in this picture is from Dalat, Sarawak. It is estimated to be approximately three hundred years old. The hole made at the upper part of the *Kelideng* accommodated the jar containing the remains of the corpse. While erecting a *Kelideng,* a slave was normally buried alive underneath the post. Another was tied to the *Kelideng* until he died of starvation. The spirits of the two slaves were believed to clear the way for the deceased to enter the World of the Dead, called *Likou Matai.*

This post has been re-erected near the government office at Dalat, Sarawak.

Above: A *Kelideng* re-erected in the compound of the Sarawak Museum.

Right: Picture of designs done on an armlet, and two equipment used in mat-making. The armlet was made from a sea shell, while the equipment, from deer horns.

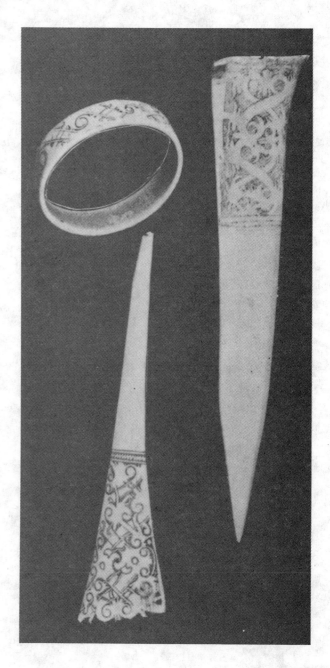

A ladder with a human head design. The 'head' is believed to be able to ward off evil spirits and diseases so that they will not disturb the longhouse's occupants. On completion of the construction of such a ladder, a ceremony called *Miring*, consisting of making an offering of food, tobacco, areca nuts and cigarettes is conducted. Some people believe that the number of steps or notches of the ladder should be made odd; an even number will bring bad luck to the occupants of the house.

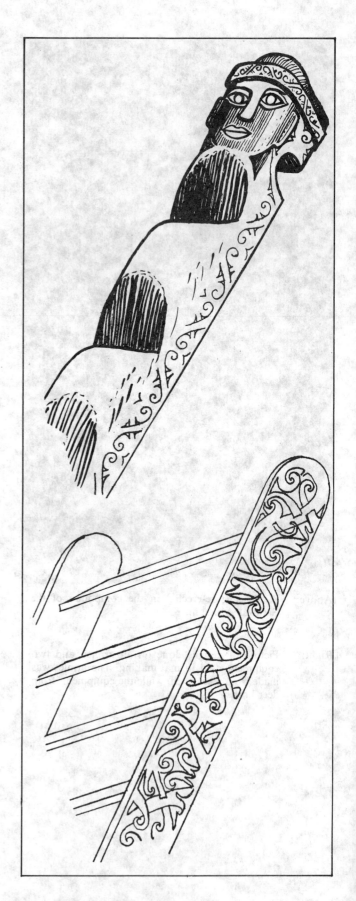

A ladder design.

Carved figure on the bow of a boat. Formerly it was quite common to see boats, especially war-boats, decorated with designs. Dragon designs were usually preferred; with the head at the bow and the tail at the stern. The dragon was supposed to drive away malignant water spirits.

A ceiling design.

Even common tools such as a paddle, pestle and mortar and a rice-miller can be decorated with designs.

PADDLE

PESTLE
MORTAR

MILLER

Nowadays Dayak shields are only used for decorative purposes. On the left is a pair of identically decorated shields.

Below are illustrations of applications of designs on three instruments: (a) the *sulat* (mat-making tool); (b) *pemisit* (implement for pulling and cramming woven strips); and (c) *lungga pengeraut* (a long-handled paring knife).

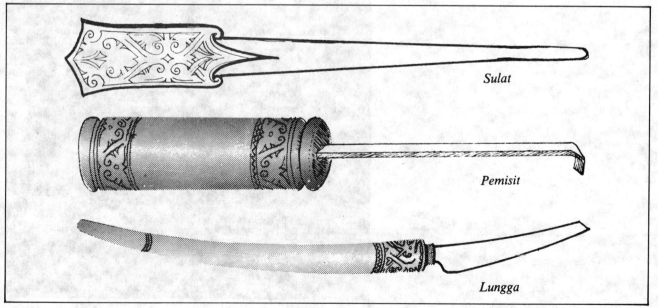

Sulat

Pemisit

Lungga

Above: A table and a chair may also be decorated with
           designs.

Below: Modern vases with Dayak designs.

A hat decorated with hornbill feathers and beads.

A wooden mask in the shape of a wild boar's head.

A picture showing some vases produced by several pottery factories in Kuching, Sarawak.

A flower vase.

Other than being applied on wood, traditional designs can be printed on materials like clothes, tablecloths, pillow cases, curtains and many others.

A piece of material after it has been printed by utilising the lino board method.

There are two methods of printing traditional designs on clothes or materials. Firstly, by using the lino board; secondly, the silk screen method. The silk screen method is more practical because its prints appear level and clean. The material affected remains soft after application. However, in the lino board method both the floral prints and the material will be a bit hard and undulating.

Some lino boards bearing designs.

A handicraft exhibition.

An arch erected at the entrance of the Agricultural
Training Centre at Long Lama, Baram, Sarawak.

The designs made on the wall of the Orang Ulu Association's House, Kuching, by Mr. Tusau Padan, a noted Kenyah designer.

Above: Designs done on the right wall of the chapel at
Long San, Marudi, Sarawak.

Below: Designs made on the left wall of the same chapel.

Above: Wall designs found at the Orang Ulu Association's
         House, Kuching, Sarawak.

Below: The hornbill design.

Left: A three-dimensional wooden tendril designs of Kenyah origin.

Below: A type of basket used by a Kayan-Kenyah mother for carrying a baby on her back.

Another type of basket for carrying a baby, decorated with coloured beads and shells.

Pierced tendril carving placed on the top of a model of a ceremonial hut.

The picture of a grandstand formerly located at the Central Padang, Kuching, Sarawak.

[a]

[b]

[c]

[a] A design-decorated guitar.
[b] A flower vase.
[c] A dragon and monkey wood-carving.

A design incorporating dragon, tigers and birds.

Above: This post is decorated with the tendril designs.

Right: A bamboo container called *bungkan buloh*, used for keeping cigarettes and tabacco. It stands on a carved wooden stand.

Above: Wall design found at the residence of the former Curator of the Sarawak Museum, the late Mr. Benedict Sandin. It comprises the trunk design and further elaborated by human being, bird and monkey forms.

Below: A decorated *sape* guitar.

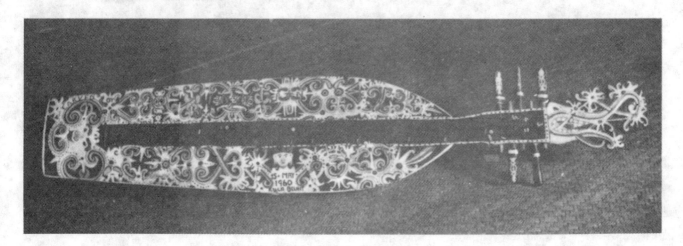

Right: This black and white shield design is made by the author himself.

Far right: Kenyah paring knives with carved horn handles.

Below: Handicrafts at the Sarawak Arts Council's stall exhibited in an exposition in Kuala Lumpur in 1972.

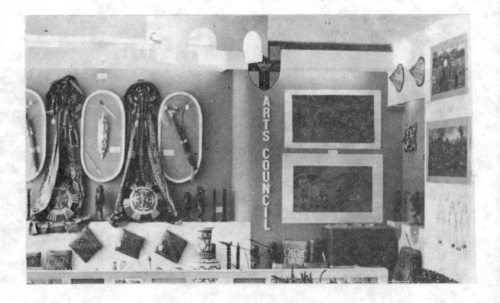

In the olden days this type of house was used by the Kayan/Kenyah tribes for storing items like gongs and padi. The model above is situated close to a government office in Marudi, Sarawak.

Above: The wooden image of a dragon found at the house of
the former Curator of the Sarawak Museum, the late
Mr. Benedict Sandin.

Below: The wooden image of a dragon hung up for
decoration at the old Kuching Airport.

This *Kelirieng* burial pole belonged to a chief of the Belaga Kayan. It stored the remains of the chief's beloved daughter. It is now re-erected near the Sarawak Museum building, Kuching.

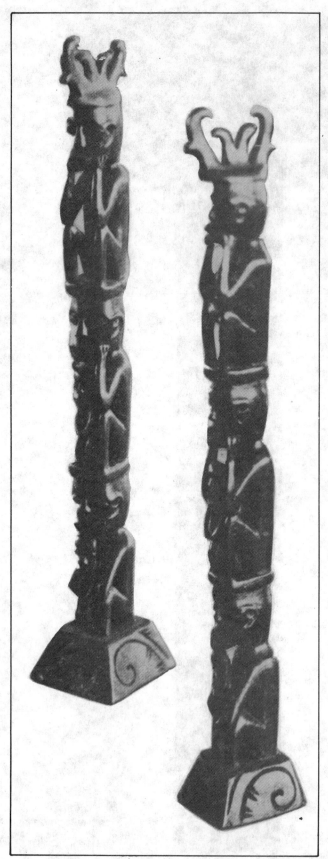

Above: This design served as a decorative piece at an agricultural exhibition held in Sibu in 1974. It was re-exhibited at a similar exhibition in Miri, Sarawak, in 1975.

Left: Iban wood carvings.

Left: This wood carving is entitled "Seringkong Carrying a Rice Mortar from the Lanjang Hill".

Below: A room at the old Kuching Airport complete with designs.

A wood-carving depicting a man carrying a dragon.
It symbolises an association between a man and a dragon.
Some legends tell us of men being bestowed with magical
powers by dragons.

Left: A bamboo container for keeping pens or pencils.

Below: Various exhibits like neckties, woven and embroidered materials, baskets, etc., made by members of a former 4-H Club, Sarawak. These were displayed at a handicraft exhibition organised by the Club. Most of the designs in the exhibits are Bent Designs.

Formerly when a high-ranking Kayan died the corpse was kept temporarily in a hut. After a lapse of time the bones were picked up and stored inside a jar, which was the placed in a specially constructed small hut called *salong*. Finally the *salong* was placed at the top of the *kelirieng* burial pole. Each event involved lavish ceremonies.

Shown above is the picture of a *salong* which was placed at the top of the *kelirieng* burial pole now re-erected near the Sarawak Museum building, Kuching.

Photograph of Kenyah designs which were once erected at the entrance to the Sarawak Museum. The designs were done on plywood by two noted Museum designers, Mr. Tusau Padan and Mr. Tubau.

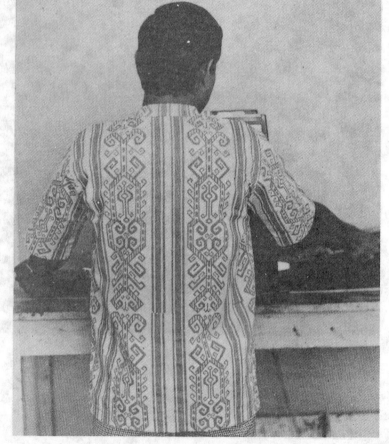

Above: Printed designs using the lino board method.

Right: This person is wearing a shirt printed with the silk screen method. It was done by the author himself.

The Bidayuh bamboo designs are similar to some Iban designs. Such designs are used to decorate bamboo containers, which are popular especially among tourists.

Right: A type of container known as *Mpulok Nkannuh* in Bidayuh. It is made from bamboo and used for keeping food.

Below: A small ritual wooden shield called *Papan Dayung Pancha*. This shield is used by the medicine women in a special ceremony to protect a baby from any evil.

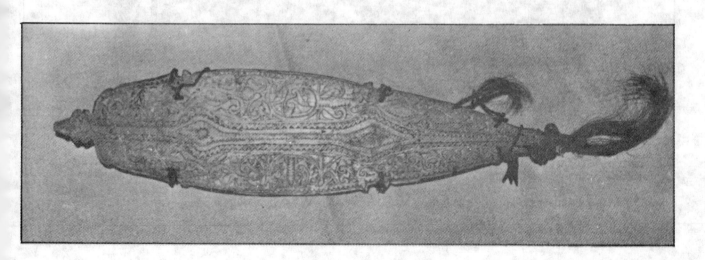

[a]

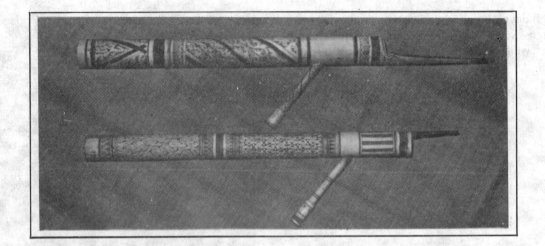

[b]

[c]

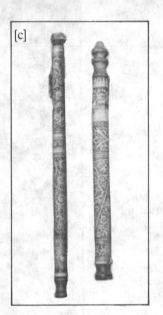

[d]

[e]

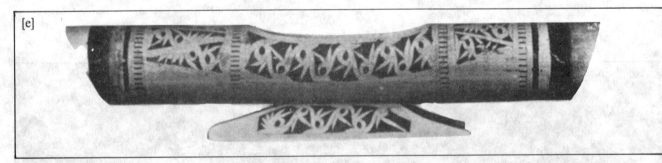

[a] This *pengudut* bamboo pipe for smoking tobacco is decorated with the Leaf Design.

[b] A tool for crushing areca nut and betel leaf *(gobek)*.

[c] A bamboo container called *Buruh Aping*, used for storing oil. It is used by medicine men during a healing ceremony.

[d] A bamboo container for storing lime; the lime to be chewed together with areca nut and betel leaf.

[e] A bamboo ashtray.

330

Above: A bamboo pencil container.

Left: A bamboo coin-container. The main designs of both
        containers began from 'J' Curves.

This is a Malay knife known as *badik*, used as a weapon. The silver handle and scabbard bear authentic Malay designs.

A sun-hat made from leaves. The rim is decorated with red cloth and white buttons. The middle is adorned with a star-shaped design ornamented with coloured beads.

A richly-decorated land float paraded in Sarikei, Sarawak, on the occasion of the King's Birthday Celebration in 1982. On the right are designs made on the side of the float.

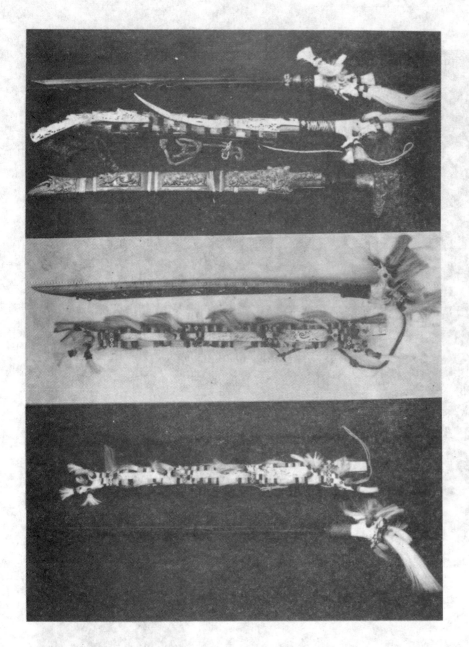

Like the Ibans, the Kenyahs are also skilful in making knives. The knife blades are normally decorated with pierced and incised designs. The handles are normaly made of deer horns, and the scabbards of hardwood. Both are elaborately carved. In the photograph below, the knife with its handle unadorned with hair is made by an Iban, while the rest are made by the Kenyahs.

A bottle may also be decorated with designs.

Left: An uncomplicated scaly dragon design.

334

In the olden days, some of Sarawak's indigenous peoples were fond of decorating the doors of their houses with designs. On the left are photographs of such doors.

Carved animal figures.

A table decorated with tendril design. Four carved animal figures form the legs.

CHAPTER 12

COMMENTS ON DESIGNS

AFTER having done my research on certain aspects of Dayak designs, and putting down the various approaches as outlined in this book, I personally feel that for the betterment of Dayak culture the correct methods of designing should be adhered to. Designs done improperly are a mockery to the Dayak art of designing. Nowadays Dayak designs are gaining popularity despite the fact that some designs have lost certain elements of their originality and authenticity. Authoritative bodies should be established to monitor the standard, authenticity and development of Dayak designs, as is the case with Malay designs in Peninsular Malaysia.

However, it is indeed heartening to note that Dayak designs are making appearances on arches, public buildings, handicrafts, greeting cards and others. I give credit to the artists for articulating their efforts in various forms and media. I hope that modern artists of Dayak designs will make use of the methods and techniques described in this book which took me years to compile.

Nowadays many houses are decorated with designs. However, many of the designs lack identity. One cannot tell whether they are of Malay, Dayak or Chinese origin. Some artists are under the impression that Dayak designs are simple, thus easy to create. Such an assumption is certainly untrue.

Below is a photograph of a section of metal fence of the Kuching Municipal Council's Aquarium. We notice that the design comprise the 'S', 'J' and 'V' Curves. Although the design is not of Dayak origin, it does bear semblance to one, except that the curves have not been given sufficient elaboration.

MASYARAKAT ADIL KEBANGSAAN MIRARA

Notice the middle part of the arch's designs. It looks like an uprooted tapioca plant with its tubers sticking out. Some of the leaves resemble sweet potato leaves with contorted shapes. The curve used is not clearly shown, but it is probably a mixture of the 'J' and 'S' Curves. The overall layout is quite commendable, though it can be improved as follows:

This is an improvement of the design on the left. In fact there are many ways of improving it.

This shield replica was one of the several that was often used as a decoration at the entrance to the Central Padang, Kuching, on several grand celebrations. At first glance the design looks perfect. Let us examine the type of leaf and rhomb patterns used. Most of the leaves are rounded at the tips. This is uncharacteristic of Dayak designs. Modification can be made by altering the leaves and rhombs.

To people who do not understand much about designs, the design below is a unique piece of Dayak design. Actually it is not an authentic Dayak of Malay design.

Let us take a closer look at the upper portion in the box of the extreme right. The leaves have been misplaced and do not curve. The rhombs are too thin. However, the design can be modified without altering much of its layout.

This is a modified version of the upper portion of the design. The leaves, curves and rhombs are properly made. It can now be aptly called 'Kissing Dragon'.

This design is an effort of a designer of average skill. I wish to make a brief comment on it.

Some of the leaves can be further elaborated to fill the empty spaces, especially on the right side of the design. Part of the design at the top left side is not connected to its main body. This can be improved by extending its tail so that it joins the main design at the top left jorquette.

This is the improved version of the design.

A sun-hat made from leaves. Its rim is decorated with a piece of red cloth and white-coloured buttons. A star-shaped design made from colourful beads can be seen in the middle.

This is a traditional Kenyah *sape* guitar. The body is carved with tendril designs, and the head adorned with dragon-head carving.

The designs on the wall were done by some Iban children. Although the designs appear crude and simple, their originality remain intact. Apparently the children in the family has already developed a taste for designing, even in their early years.

Note the dwarf-like figures drawn on the wall. They resemble the figures usually made on the Iban *pua kumbu*. The other patterns also bear similarities to patterns found in Iban weavings and matworks.

GLOSSARY

ajat	a medium size plaited basket made from rattan
along	a blackish substance left behind by smoke; smuts; lamp-black; soot.
Antu Rangka	the name given to a type of design meaning "The Greedy Ghost".
baka	a type of small basket.
baju subak	a type of woven clothing.
basong	a type of basket for carrying necessaries; carried slung over the shoulder.
Baya Butang	the name given to a type of design, meaning 'Adulterous Crocodiles'.
Bedujong Bunga Ringkai	the *ringkai* flower (genus *Mitrephora reticulata*), stuck into a headress and worn as decoration.
Bekaul Kawai	a type of design.
buah pua'	the patterns of Iban cloth weavings.
buah empit	an oval-shaped fruit of a jungle tree (genus *Sterculia*).
buan	the *simpur* tree (a small tree bearing yellow flowers: genus *Dillenia*).
Buat	a term of address, meaning 'friend', 'comrade', 'pal'.
bubut	(*Contrococcyx*). A type of black coloured bird.
Bunga Terung	a type of body tattoo, 'brinjal flower'.
Bunga Terung Empat Betentang	body tattoo pattern based on the shape of brinjal flowers.
Bungkan buluh	bamboo cylinder used as a container.
Bunsu Rabing Mangah Gayau Bedayung	the name given to a type of design meaning 'A Ferocious Young Crocodile Rowing'.
Buntak Aloi	a false name adopted by the god Keling in the story *Buntak Aloi And Buntak Rusa*.
Buntak Rusa	a false name adopted by the god Keling in the story *Buntak Aloi And Buntak Rusa*.
Burung Kenyalang	Rhinoceros Hornbill (*Buceros Rhinoceros*).
buruh aping	bamboo cylinder used as a container (Bidayuh).
Chandi	a carved structure for placing the wooden image of the Rhinoceros Hornbill during the *Gawai Kenyalang* (Hornbill Festival) ceremony.
Chunggit (Chunggit Dudul; Chunggit Semunjing; Chunggit Juring)	a type of sharp-pointed pattern in an Iban traditional design.
Dulang Ini Manang	the name given to a type of design, meaning 'Tray Belonging to the goddess Ini Manang.'
Dulang Simpandai	the name given to a type of design meaning, "Tray Belonging To the god Simpandai".
Dejai	a type of design.
empili	a type of jungle tree (genus *Lithocarpus*).
empit	the 'empit' tree (genus *Sterculia*).
engkerumong	a set of small gongs (usually eight).
Entadu Berasok	the name given to a type of design, meaning 'Entwining Caterpillars'.
Entegulun	a type of design applied on the back of the hand of an Iban warrior who had succeeded in slaying his anemies.
Entuyut	a type of design based on the shape of the pitcher plant or 'Monkey-cup Creeper' (genus *Nepenthes*).
gawai	religious rites accompanied by festivities; feast or festival.
Gawai Kenyalang	Hornbill Ritual Festival, named after the wooden figure of a Rhinoceros Hornbill used in the rites.
Gelayan Ragak Riang	the name of an inhabitant of the godly longhouse called 'Gelong Batu Nakong'.
Gerama Murong	the name give to a type of design based on the shape of a crab.
Gerasi Papa Saum Nyawa	the name given to a type of design, meaning "Two giants with a mouth".
Gelong (also Gelong Batu Nakong)	another heavenly kingdom of Iban gods and goddesses.
ijok	a type of palm (genus Arenga pinnata).
Jabai Nyuntai	the name given to a type of design, orginating from the shape of the leaves of a fig tree species (genus *Ficus*).
Jagu Bekaul Iko	a type of design, meaning 'Crocodiles with locked tails'.

Janggut Undai	a type of design, meaning 'Prawn's Feelers'.
Jelenga Udun	a type of design, meaning 'A Notch'.
jempul	a type of sword.
jerenang	a type of red dye obtained from the fruit of a large rotan species (genus Daemonorops).
jerunei	a huge pole, decorated with designs, specifically made for storing the remains of Melanau aristocrats in the old days.
kain pandak	a type of woven short skirt formerly worn by Iban maidens.
Kala Bejagang	a type of design, meaning 'Scorpion at the Ready'.
Kamba Nanggong	the name given to type of woven design or pattern meaning 'The Kamba Elf Lifting Something'.
kayau	a raid; a foray; a war.
keladan	a timber tree (genus *Dryobalanops oblongifera*).
kelambi kubal	a short sleeveless war-coat worn during battle in the olden days.
Keling	one of the Iban gods, well-reputed for his authority, leadership, heroism, etc. He possesses various nicknames (e.g. Keling Gerasi Nading; Keling Gerasi Nading Bujang Berani Kempang; etc.).
Kelingai	tattooed patterns applied on the body, usually on the back, forearm and thigh.
Kelingai Bunga Terung	tattooed patterns originating from the shape of the brinjal flower.
Kelingai Ketam Bedayung	tattooed patterns, meaning 'The Rowing Crab'.
Kelingai Ketam Ngerayap	tattooed paterns, meaning 'The Crawling Crab'.
Kelingai Tabak	tattooed patterns originating from the shape of a brass tray.
Kelirieng	similar in concept and form to the *Jerunei*, as explained before, except that the keliriengs were used by the Kayan, Punan and Skapan communities.
kenyalang	the Rhinoceros Hornbill (*Buceros Rhinoceros*).
kepayang	a tree yielding edible fruit (genus Pangium edule).
Kera Rakang	the name given to a type of woven design originating from the animal shape.
Ketam Ngerayap	please refer to the explanation as given in Kelingai *Ketam Ngerayap* above.
Kilat Nyelar	a connotation meaning "Lightning Strikes".
Kumang	an Iban goddess who is well-reputed for her beauty and authority; she is the wife of the god Keling.
ladong	a stout round basket fitted with shoulder straps made of bark, normally carried over the shoulder.
Laja	another Iban god believed to reside at the heavenly abode of Panggau Libau. Laja also possesses various nicknames, e.g. Laja Tampak Moa; Laja Tampak Moa Nakang Jerenang; etc.
lanji	a tall and big rottan basket meant for carrying padi.
lapak	a white patch found at the surface of the flesh of the *kepayang* fruit.
leka pelian	a lengthy invocation chanted by a medicine-man (*manang*), during a curing rite for the sick.
lelaih	a species of river fish.
lemambang	an Iban bard who is an expert in ritual chants.
Likau Matai	the world of the dead (according to traditional Melanau belief).
Lua Genali Bekaul Kaki	the name given to a type of design meaning "The Water Spirit With Interlocking Feet".
Lulong	one of the goddesses residing at the heavenly kingdom of Panggau Libau, the wife of god Laja. She is also renowned for her beauty and power.
lungun	a coffin.
Menyeti Bali Betangkai	the name given to a pattern found in an Iban cloth weaving (*pua kumbu*).
mpulok nkannuh	a type of container made from bamboo (Bidayuh).
Ngelai	one of the gods residing at the godly kingdom of Gelong.
ngayap	courting a maiden at her house at night.
paku kelindu	a large fern species (genus Blechnum orientale L.)
Pala Numbing	a type of design said to be based on the shape of the head of a giant.
Pala Rusa	a type of design resembling the deer's head.
papan dayung	a small wooden shield used in a Bidayuh ritual ceremony.
papan pengap/papan turai	a narrow piece of board with picture symbols drawn·on its surface, for teaching Iban ritual chants.

Pandak Sagatak	one of the inhabitants of the celestial abode of Panggau Libau.
Panggau Libau	a celestial abode of Iban gods and goddesses.
Pasun Nyalak Di Lebak Tanah Emperan, **Pasun Tunggal Ngigal Ngaki Karangan**	a type of design, meaning 'The Giant's Dog Barks At The Lembah Flatlands, The Solitary Dog Barks At the Edge of the Pebble Beach'.
pelai	a soft light wood tree (genus Alstonia).
pemanis	a love charm or potion.
pemisit	a claw-like instrument used for cramming the woven strips in mat-making.
pengap	lengthy invocations chanted by several experts (*lemambang*) in various healing and ritual ceremonies.
pentik	a carved wooden image set to ward off evil.
piring	an offering of food, tobacco and betel nut served to dieties.
pua kumbu	ritual clothes or blankets of various types and importance woven by Iban ladies.
purang	a type of tree
raga	a small type of basket with a narrow bottom and oval rim, carried slung with straps over the shoulders.
Rajang Merundai	the name given to a type of design meaning "The 'Rajang' Orchid Hangs Suspended".
Rajang Segempong	the name given to a type of design meaning "A Cluster Of The 'Rajang' Orchid".
Rengguang	the name given to a type of design originating from the shape of a brown arthropod about 2 inches long that curls up when touched.
ruai	the Argus Pheasant bird (*Argusianus argus L.*).
Sabang Seluang	a palm-like plant normally used in various Iban ritual ceremonies.
sadau	the upper storey, 'upstairs', especially loft of a longhouse reached by steps from the main room.
sala	a type of tree (genus *Canarium*).
salong	a small carved and decorated funerary hut meant for storing jars containing the bones of people of the upper class in olden days (practised by the Kayans, Punans, Sekapans, and some other indigenous groups).
Sandah Ngua	the name given to a type of design meaning 'A Cricket Singing a Ritual Song'.
semawa	a design originating from the shape of a flying fox.
semunjing	a plant species.
Sengalang Burung	A Bird Diety and a God of War, possessing the highest power of authority, according to Iban belief.
sengkerong buah empit	elliptical shapes of the *empit* fruit.
Sepungga Lumpong Nanga	another of the Iban dieties.
Simpurai Muntigerai Sepatu Manok Antu	another Iban diety from the heavenly abode of Panggau Libau. He is famous for his strength and heroism.
sulat	a bone needle or bodkin used in mat-making.
sungkup	a miniature house erected over the grave, decorated with certain designs. It is erected during the Gawai Antu Festival.
tajau	certain types of large glazed earthenware jars, much valued by Bornean natives in the olden days.
takin	a type of small basket usually carried by women.
tanju	a roofless platform built at the front part of a longhouse.
tarum	a species of plant (genus *Indigofera*); a blue-black dye, usually for dyeing threads to be woven, can be made from its leaves.
Tedong Beambai	a type of design, meaning 'Cobra in Love'.
Tedong Ngelantar	a nickname meaning 'sliding Cobra'.
teku	bends and curves (concerning design shapes).
tiang kelirieng	please refer to the explanation as given for kelirieng.
timpa	a large basket
tirok	a spike spear without barb for probing turtle under water.
tungkat lemambang	a type of staff or walking stick decorated with designs, used by a bard during invocations in various healing and cultural rites.
tunjang	stilt tree root or any angular protrusion, e.g., points woven on basket or cap.
Ukir Teku	Bent Design.
Undai Beradai	a type of design originating from the shape of a prawn.

347